Sandbox Society

Sandbox Society

EARLY EDUCATION IN BLACK AND WHITE AMERICA:

Sally Lubeck

 The Falmer Press

(A Member of the Taylor & Francis Group)
London and Philadelphia

UK   The Falmer Press, Falmer House, Barcombe, Lewes, East Sussex, BN8 5DL

USA   The Falmer Press, Taylor & Francis Inc., 242 Cherry Street, Philadelphia, PA 19106-1906

Copyright © Sally Lubeck 1985

First published in 1985

Library of Congress Cataloging in Publication Data

Lubeck, Sally.
  Sandbox society.

  Bibliography: p.
  Includes index.
  1. Education, Preschool—Middle West—Cross-cultural studies. 2. Project Head Start (U.S.)—Cross-cultural studies. 3. Child rearing—Middle East—Cross-cultural studies. I. Title.
LB1140.24.M53L8   1985   372′.21′0977   85-10422
ISBN 1-85000-051-4
ISBN 1-85000-050-6 (pbk.)

Typeset in 11/13 Caledonia by
Imago Publishing Ltd, Thame, Oxon

Printed in Great Britain by Taylor & Francis (Printers) Ltd, Basingstoke

Contents

Tables and Figures

Table

Figure

The great gift that members of the human race have for each other is not exotic experiences but an opportunity to achieve awareness of the structure of their *own* system, which can be accomplished only by interacting with others who do not share that system — members of the opposite sex, different age groups, different ethnic groups, and different cultures ... The rules governing behavior and structure of one's own cultural system can be discovered only in a specific context or real-life situation.

Edward Hall
Beyond Culture

There are two primary moments in the constitution of a general anthropology: interest in other peoples and their way of life, and concern to explain them within a frame of reference that includes ourselves.

Dell Hymes
Reinventing Anthropology

Acknowledgements

A book is a product not so much of a person as of people and of a time. With this book this is especially true, for it was forged out of much wondering and soul-searching on my part, but stimulated by the hard questions and gentle encouragement of others, and, especially, by the opportunity to share in the lives of the people which it portrays.

Lou Smith was the first person to introduce me to the perspective of ethnography. In the earliest stages, through the pilot study and on into the fieldwork, he was a source of inspiration and encouragement. With his great gift of seeing flowers in seeds and of nourishing ideas only half-formed, his classes, his comments, and the comments of his students were invaluable. Thanks also go to David Smith and to Claire Woods-Elliot, whom I visited early in the fieldwork. Seldom does one feel 'heard' by relative strangers, but they listened at a critical time. Claire shared with me experiences that helped me to re-form what it was I was about, and David gave me insights into the effects of my own enculturation that made me determined to change the course of my enquiry. What understanding was gained from the fieldwork experience is due in part to their brief but powerful influence.

The study was originally written as a thesis at the University of Missouri-Saint Louis, and I am grateful for the fellowship and assistance I received there. I would like once again to thank the members of my committee: Jon Marshall, Chuck Fazzaro, Jim Walter and Murray Wax. In the best empiricist tradition, they never allowed me to settle into platitudes but always insisted that I observe and describe. I am particularly indebted to Jon Marshall, who carved out a path so that an alternative research approach could find its way.

It was Murray Wax who first apprehended that I was asking cultural questions, questions fundamental to anthropology. He helped me to grapple with the literature, offered books that collapsed old systems and forced me to re-structure new ones, and read and re-read drafts far beyond the cause of duty. He has been for years a wise and learned teacher and a good friend. Thanks also go to Rosalie who, in our brief and stolen lunches, helped me ponder what it means to be a woman in all its complexities. Finally, I wish to thank Courtney Cazden who graciously read a chapter of the manuscript in its final throes and who offered helpful suggestions. Very special thanks are due to her for the opportunity to take the questions further in a year of postdoctoral study. Though the ideas contained herein should not be construed to represent the positions of the people I have named, I am deeply grateful for their influence.

I would also like to acknowledge the assistance of Thomas Jordan, Dean of the Graduate School and Vice-Chancellor of Research at UMSL, who provided me with a job on his child development project, support for mine, and the opportunity over the years to talk about child development, broadly conceived. He has been responsible, to a great extent, for the fact that the study has found its way into print. Finally, thanks are due to Malcolm Clarkson, Managing Director of the Falmer Press, whose encouragement — and deadlines! — have kept me to the task.

I have also appreciated deeply the help of family and friends. But very special thanks are due for the support of my parents, Lambert and Erma Jean Roy, and for that of my sister, Kay, who has given generously of her time to help with children and chores, to Dennis whose influence is marked in the finding of the question, and to Alec, whose disagreeing has been thought-provoking and whose agreeing has been needed and valued. It has been important to know a father who mothers.

I am especially grateful to the women in the Head Start Center and to those in the preschool for sharing with me their lives and work and for helping me with patience and humor to understand, in some small measure, what it is we are about. It is to them, and to the children in our care, that I dedicate this book.

Sally Lubeck
March, 1985

Prologue

Overview

It is commonly believed that racial and social class differences in achievement and/or in ability *cause* inequality, that is, because poor and minority children don't do well in school, they fail to gain access to the opportunities available in society. This book suggests that a case can be made for the alternative thesis: that inequality causes differences.

The book has two main purposes. The first is to understand how those poor and black have adapted to a distinctive social history and how these adaptations are reproduced in a black Head Start classroom and transmitted to the next generation. The second is to understand the processes by which white middle-class or what is commonly called 'mainstream' culture is adopted and how these processes differ, through a description and analysis of a white preschool less than a mile away. Both programs are located within one of the first communities in the nation that has attempted to foster a fair housing policy and desegregated schools.

A History

It is an oddity of life that we frequently consider people around us, those 'different' from ourselves, as 'problems' or 'threats' (and that we are so considered), while, at the same time, we are capable of mustering much interest and compassion for those far away — those in Selma, or Central America, or Africa. There is a tendency to discount our own history and our own place in history.

In the course of writing this book, I have had to reconstruct the history of the people with whom I worked, people who shared my community but not my ways, people who reared children in ways different from my own. My reactions to our differences have changed over time: early horror that I could see only stereotypes in what was being done 'wrong', later conviction that, if they could only be shown a (my) 'better' way, they would change, and later still appreciation for a way of life that had possibilities different from my own — and dawning realization of my own — and my own culture's — limitations.

The study that needs to be told is one that has no obvious beginning and seemingly no end, and so its rendering is but a pinprick in time. It is a story of a single city in the United States, a story of a suburb of that city, a story of two early education programs in that suburb, a story ultimately of the few people in the act of re-creating the social order by transmitting their values, attitudes and life orientations to the next generation. There, near the sandbox, in this littlest of worlds, children take in cues of who they are and of what the world they will inhabit is like.

It is a story of two histories in a city by a river: one white, one black, histories that, though interwoven in time, represent separate heritages, histories carved out of the American experience of opportunity or of enslavement. Black history tells us little and yet much. The courthouse had a slave pen on one corner, a whipping post on another. Slaves, we learn, were chained together and marched through the streets. The free black school was closed by the sheriff, another was destroyed by a mob, and in 1847 a state law made it illegal to provide schooling for free blacks and mulattoes.

The story is also one of resistance and struggle: the Freedom School on a steamboat in the river just over the state line, to which dozens of black youths rafted each day for years; the last attempt in 1861 to auction slaves from the Courthouse steps, unsuccessful because a crowd of 2000 prevented it; the 100,000 whites and 8000 blacks from the State who fought for the Union in the Civil War, and the 30,000 who fought on the Confederate side.

There is the story of the school for fugitive slaves burned by a mob in 1863; at War's end, the Radical Constitution which required that school boards support black education, and the resulting appropriation of one-fifth of one per cent of the budget to the recently formed 'Colored Board'; and the constitutional ban on mixing the races that was to keep schools 'separate and unequal' for decades to come.

In the early twentieth century conflict between the races was minimal because blacks 'knew their place'. They lived on the edges of the business district, in the river wards, or in dilapidated housing vacated by upwardly-mobile immigrant families. They were prohibited from eating in the same restaurants as whites and from staying in the same hotels. Toilet facilities and barber shops were segregated, and a separate 'peanut gallery' was designated in theatres. In 1916 voters overwhelmingly ratified a residential segregation law that prevented any one of a particular race to move to a block where 75 per cent of the residents were of another race. Though the law was never enacted (it was declared unconstitutional in 1918) legally-binding restrictive covenants subsequently were used to accomplish the same end. Black and white housing remained segregated in fact if not in law.

Migrations from the South greatly increased the numbers of blacks during World War I. Lured by the promise of industrial jobs, the movement of rural Southern blacks to the urban cities of the North became one of the major population shifts of the century. In the summer of 1917 the most violent race riot of the period took place on the east side of the river. It was fired by a company's use of black 'scab' labor to break a strike. Hundreds were wounded, hundreds of houses burned, and the total number of dead, with estimates as high as 100, was never determined. A news reporter chronicled the massacre in which black men and women were surrounded and stoned to death by whites with 'cool deliberateness and (a) spirit of fun.' Police stationed on the bridge safeguarded hundreds fleeing from the slaughter; the city, with the aid of the Red Cross and other agencies, provided them with food and shelter.

During the Depression the city had its Hooverville, small wood and tin shacks on the river, the homes of the homeless, both black and white. As farms foreclosed, many farmers made their way to the city, only to find there were no jobs to be had. By 1933 the national unemployment rate peaked at 24.9 per cent, but 30 per cent of the city's white population were jobless, and 80 per cent of its blacks were unemployed or underemployed. The reasons for the astoundingly high rate of unemployment were many. There were instances of blacks being fired, so that whites could be hired in their place. The meat-packing industry reduced its labor force by 70 per cent by laying off only black workers. Ironically, many blacks had found work because they could be paid less; when non-discrimination codes mandated that their salaries be raised, many lost their jobs. Black males, dozens with union cards from other places, were excluded from trade unions for years. They were not allowed to work as craftsmen, either when the black hospital was constructed or when black schools were built.

For decades the elite had abandoned large homes on private places as urban noise, smoke and congestion surrounded them. Poor families crowded into over-sized houses, and whole sections of the city eventually succumbed to urban blight. This pattern paralleled the national trend; the core of the city, like that of others, came to house the poorest of the poor, with many old structures in the central city having no running water or inside toilets. By 1940 80 per cent of new houses were being built in the suburbs.

Meanwhile, 'white flight' had been occurring for decades, but it accelerated as redevelopment projects leveled sections of the city and highway construction severed whole blocks of residents from their ethnic neighborhoods and churches. By 1950 blacks comprised 18 per cent of the population; by 1960, 28.8 per cent; in the interim the city's population declined 12.5 per cent. Despite the Supreme Court ruling that outlawed discrimination in housing in the 1950s, precedents already had been set. In the 1954 'Brown vs. the Board of Education of Topeka' case, the Supreme Court ruled that 'separate but equal' schools were unconstitutional, yet segregated housing continued to militate against shared educational facilities. The city had established a pattern mirrored throughout the industrial North, two cities in a city, a black northern section, a white southern one.

In the 1960s the Civil Rights movement was a key factor in heightening public awareness of racism. In 1963 and 1964 Congress passed laws which invalidated segregationist practices. Blacks, like others, were guaranteed the right to enter all public places, the right to vote, and the right to hold public office. In 1965 Congress ratified the major social policy initiative of the century. Legislation dictated that hundreds of thousands, and, over the years, millions, of poor — often minority — children be provided the same social services and educational experiences that white, middle-class children had as their birthright. These provisions were to be guaranteed early on, before they entered public schooling, so that these children might now have a 'Head Start'.

In the twilight of these events, one suburban community bordering the city began to act. Forest Hills, a pseudonym for the community that is the locus of this study, is a liberal university community. Some of its residents had been instrumental in organizing the metropolitan Freedom of Residence movement, but the most immediate impetus for local action came from the realization that black students at the university could not find a place to eat on Sundays. It was the year 1960. Though the situation was the same throughout the nation, issues of segregation, racism, and oppression came home.

Initially the community's Human Relations Commission served an instructional role by holding hearings, bringing in experts, commissioning studies, and by exposing real estate practices. Agents would not sell suburban property to blacks, so some citizens in the community began to run interference with established practices. By 1962–63 straws were buying property and turning it over to black families. Sales were effected on the northside of the city where housing was less costly. By 1963–64 panic started when one or two black families had moved onto a block. Real estate agents, in turn, seized the opportunity to make quick sales. Playing on people's fears, agents began calling residents and urging them to move quickly 'so you can still get your price.' Many elderly people on fixed incomes, on being told their property would be rendered worthless, panicked and sold to speculators who made large profits. Property values plummeted (though they rose again after the initial transition), and a steady exodus of whites left the community, despite valiant efforts that still persist to create a viable integrated community.

The panic preceded a fair housing law, though this had been the goal of those who had proceeded cautiously in the early years of the decade. Advocates believed the mandate would accomplish two ends. First, it would be a means of preventing resegregation in the northern section of the community. Secondly, it would serve as an example for other communities to do the same. In 1965, at a time when there was no national or state fair housing law, the City Council feared that a local law would create havoc. Instead the Council adopted a fair housing resolution. Initiatives sought to rely on volunteerism, to eliminate steering practices, and to rule that 'for sale' signs could not be displayed in the community. Anti-solicitation laws were passed though probably too late to have any effect. Subsequent to the resolution, no other suburban community ever attempted to adopt a fair housing policy.

By 1970 the schools on the northside were virtually segregated, all-black schools. By 1980 schools in the middle section of the city had a black majority; schools in the southern section were still predominantly white. The pattern historically characteristic of the urban North had been reproduced in microcosm. In the early 1980s, when the study on which this book is based was conducted, the median income for black American households was slightly more than half that of white households, 45 per cent of black children under 18 years of age were living below the poverty line, compared to 15 per cent of white children. In Forest Hills bussing to achieve racial 'integration' in the schools began in 1982.

What follows is the story of two programs, one a white preschool in the central section of the community, the other a black Head Start center on the northside, two classrooms in a community that tried to change the course of history, a frame in an ever-lengthening film. Yet it is also the ongoing saga of separate histories, separate futures, and, ultimately, different worlds. For history such as this is not confined to schoolbooks but rather governs our actions and defines our realistic assessment of what life holds for our children.

1   Introduction

Two preschool classrooms can look much the same. There are small tables and chairs, art easels, books, blocks — the accoutrements of an early learning setting. This book presents results of an ethnographic study which goes beyond such similarities to define differences in the processes by which children are taught, differences, that is, in the way in which child rearers transfer their values and life experiences to children in school settings.

Statement of the Problem

The study is a controlled comparison of two classrooms similar in size and in the equipment provided. The classrooms are located in different neighbourhoods of an older suburb of an American city. The major differences between the two settings are in terms of social class and race. In the Head Start Center, teachers and students are black; in the preschool, teachers and students are white.

Conducted over the period of one school year, the study uses an anthropological perspective to look at the day-to-day processes by which adults teach children to adapt to the reality which they themselves experience. As Hess (1970) has stated it, the problem can be formulated as a series of questions:

> What external conditions influence childrearers? What adaptations do people make to these conditions? How are these adaptations conveyed to children? And what behaviours do children manifest as a consequence?

The settings are looked at not so much as classrooms as they are 'windows' through which to observe the child rearing strategies of two sets of women who have grown up in different cultures. As such, the study has two major dimensions. One is to reconstruct and describe ways in which child rearing strategies differ. The other is to indicate how these practices are meaningful and consonant with the teachers' cultural experiences outside the school.

The study is concerned with schools that are continuous with family life and therefore special as schools. In both cases the teachers are mothers in families very like those of the children they teach. Their values and attitudes reflect different cultural heritages based partly on belief but importantly based in the historical, economic and logistical conditions of their lives. These same realities continue to influence their behaviour during the school day. Beliefs about what is best for children and what is expected of them are born out of these experiences, yet there are also structural differences in the job definitions of the two sets of teachers that press them in the same direction as the logistical character of their lives at home — with the Head Start women having heavier and more diverse responsibilities.

Issues

In the last twenty years educational research has focused increasing attention on the problem of 'difference'. Researchers have sought not only to define the nature of the problem — what accounts for cognitive and behavioral differences between the races — but also to define what can/should be done about those differences.

There are four dominant perspectives of the causes and consequences of differences between poor Black children and those more generally within the mainstream of society; the biological, the environmental, the social structural, and the cultural.

Biological

The first view, propounded or assumed for centuries, was a case for the heritability of intelligence. Differences among individuals were seen to be the result of different — genetically determined — abilities. In the Old South and later during Reconstruction and the early twentieth century, most southern whites believed in the biological inferiority of the Negro. Such a belief served to sustain the pro-slavery argument — that slavery provided food, shelter, and care to a people unable to care

2

for themselves. Though black scholars decried this view, it was many years before mainstream historians seriously questioned its validity (Smith, 1980).

Historically in America, differences in achievement were linked to differences in ability. The pervasive American belief in rugged individualism and the 'self-made man,' rooted as it was in the Puritan ethic, reinforced the conviction that those who did well had earned their reward and were thereby favored by God. By the same token, those who did not succeed were frequently considered merely lazy, or, for the more religious, as disenfranchised by God. In the 1920s and 1930s the assumption of a biological meritocracy became joined to the notion of differential biological worth. The popular eugenics movement thus helped to promote policies of racial segregation, immigration restriction, and student classification (Selden, 1983).

The most controversial and widely-publicized statement of the belief in the genetic basis of intelligence was Jensen's (1969) article which attempted to demonstrate that there were significant racial group differences in intelligence and that these differences were genetically based.[1] Jensen contended that genetic factors were more important than environmental factors in the determination of individual differences in IQ. Basing his argument on statistical analysis of existing data, he maintained that 80 per cent of the IQ variance was due to genetic factors; 20 per cent was presumed to be due to environmental differences.

Jensen noted that on tests of abstract thinking and problem-solving blacks typically scored 15 points lower than whites or Orientals. He made a case that such differences were an indication of different gene populations. His major argument was based on studies of identical twins, especially on Cyril Burt's (since discredited) study of 100 pairs of identical twins in England. He also, however, cited over 100 twin and kinship studies that supported his case and 400 major IQ studies that evidenced the substantially lower IQ of American Blacks.

Extrapolating from such data, Jensen saw race as a 'breeding population,' suggesting that during slavery blacks were selected for their physical rather than mental ability. In the process of selective mating, higher order thinking never had the opportunity to develop (Edson, 1969).[2]

Though his work has received a good deal of criticism (many writers have questioned his over-reliance on IQ tests, the cultural bias of such measures, and the inability to control for environmental factors), Jensen has remained staunch in his conviction that education will not make a significant difference in the lives of Black people. According to Jensen, the problem is not merely a matter of learning but of neural structures in the brain. Eugenic planning and marriage controls would need to be instituted to have any effect on the causes and consequences of differences between Black and White Americans.

Environmental

Basing his speculations on Hebb's animal deprivation studies, Hunt (1961, 1964 and 1969) provided evidence for the alternative argument in the 'nature-nurture' controversy — that minority children were not genetically inferior, but rather environmentally deprived. The argument was supported by studies which demonstrated the effects of different environments on children (Skeels and Dye, 1939; Skeels, 1966; Kirk, 1954) and by comparative studies of twins raised together and apart (Bloom, 1964).[3]

Unlike the biological determinists who believed that individuals became what they were born to become, environmental determinists saw a cause for social action. If poor children whose lives were muted by disadvantage could be provided adequate stimulation early in life, then their lives could be transformed and the spiraling circle of poverty interrupted.

Though there had been occasional governmental initiatives to improve the lot of the poor since the Depression Era, President Johnson's 'War on Poverty' became the first attempt to use educational agencies to address problems of poverty and the unequal distribution of opportunity and resources. Education, for the first time, was to be 'compensatory'.

As a central part of the federal government's anti-poverty policies, egalitarian reform movements spearheaded education programs that focused on training poor, frequently minority women to raise children properly (Weikart and Lambie, 1964; Gray and Klaus, 1965; Levenstein, 1970 and 1972; Madden, Levenstein and Levenstein, 1976; Karnes *et al*, 1970; Gordon *et al*, 1975 and 1977; Brophy, 1970) and on early schooling programs such as Head Start and Follow Through which sought to provide children with vital educational experiences 'lacking' in their homes.[4]

Such efforts were infused with good intent, but critics were quick to note the problems. The underlying assumption that poor children were 'culturally deprived'[5] was normative in essence, imbuing minority child rearing practices with negative connotations (Wax and Wax,

1963/71; Keddie, 1973; LaBelle, 1971; Leacock, 1971). At its most extreme black families were considered 'pathological' (Moynihan, 1965), black mothers 'deficient' (see, for example, Baratz and Baratz, 1970) and a disproportionate number of Black children were labeled 'retarded'.[6]

Since environment was narrowly defined as what happened in the home, such thinking tended to place the blame on mothers and on families. The 'cause' of poor achievement was seen to reside in disadvantaged families whose members deprived their offspring of adequate stimulation. Black children did poorly in school, dropped out early, and experienced the lifelong crippling effects of environmentally-induced deficiencies.

Minority child rearing practices — what happened in the home — were thus defined as deviant by definition. If the causes and consequences of differences between black and white Americans were to be addressed, minority parents and children needed to change. Others argued, however, that such a stance was nothing less than 'blaming the victim' (Ryan, 1971).

Social Structural

Proponents of the third view have maintained that problems of poverty are not due to the individual deficiencies of the poor but rather to institutional structures that create and maintain social inequality (Baratz and Baratz, 1970; deLone, 1979; Keniston, 1977). These writers conceive of 'environment' as the entire social system in which people's lives are embedded.

Institutions are stratified and serve to maintain those in power, and schools, in turn, are structured to reward those with certain skills. Early on, teachers replicate the social class system by rewarding high SES students with good grades while low SES students receive poor marks, more criticism and less attention. At least one researcher has pointed out the economic utility of having a strata of low-achievers who move without expectation into low-status occupations (Henry, 1963).

The bell-shaped curve is seen as the visual manifestation of a social system premised on an unequal distribution of resources. Educational institutions perpetuate social inequalities (Bowles and Gintis, 1976) and teachers themselves are seen as playing an instrumental role in the stratification process (Rist, 1970 and 1978; Becker, 1971, Anyon, 1980). Others have contended that schools have little control over factors that matter, so that changing schools cannot be expected to change society (Jencks, 1972).

If the question of differences is to be addressed and minorities are to achieve anything like social and economic equality, then implicit in both stances is the assumption that, not only the schools but the society generally will have to be radically changed.

Cultural

The cultural perspective differs from the previous ones in certain critical respects. Unlike the biological argument, the relative importance of environmental over genetic factors is assumed. Unlike the environmental position, however, those who subscribe to a cultural point of view hold that there is not one normative process of growth and learning to which all peoples bend. Rather different cultural groups have developed different adaptive strategies over time, and an order and logic informs the practices of people who have lived under distinctive environmental conditions.[7] Finally, unlike the social structural position, contemporary researchers tend not to depict minorities within complex societies (or peoples in Third World countries) as pawns helpless against powerful forces beyond their control. By describing the adaptive strategies by which groups persevere under adverse conditions, people are seen as active agents in the structuring of a life that is meaningful and shared.

Although American Black families were defined for a time as inferior and 'lacking' in certain vital respects, recent writers have shown the family structure and kinship networks of Afro-Americans to be highly supportive, resilient, and functionally adaptive. Born of slavery and oppression, Afro-American culture nontheless maintained the interdependency and sense of collective responsibility of its African heritage, while, at the same time adopting aspects of white American society (Nobles, 1974; Sudarkasa, 1981). Kinship networks have been maintained so that people can survive poverty and prejudice by helping one another. Children are frequently raised in an intergenerational system of family, neighbors and friends (Hill, 1972); tasks and resources are shared (Stack, 1975); and cooperation rather than competition among members is encouraged. These values support 'taken-for-granted' child rearing practices that are recreated in an early education setting. Child training practices have been shown to be dramatically different in a white preschool setting (Lubeck, 1984).

Because the system of socialization is profoundly different, some researchers have argued that Black children develop a different orientation to life, a tendency to respond to things in terms of the whole rather than its parts (Hilliard, 1976), person rather than object orientation

(Young, 1970), and relational thinking rather than abstract thinking (Shade, 1982; Cohen, 1969/76).

Though highly functional within the black kinship network, these strategies may not prepare children to adapt to the specific requirements of American schooling. Numerous writers have shown that there is continuity between home and school environments for white, middle-class children, but that black and other minority children experience profound cultural discontinuity upon entering school (Cohen, 1969/76; Dumont and Wax, 1969; Byers and Byers, 1972; Erickson and Mohatt, 1982; Heath, 1982, 1983; Philips, 1983). Various solutions have been offered: that children be taught to be bilingual and bicultural (Valentine, 1971), so that they can both maintain their ethnic identity and accrue the benefits of functioning within the society at large, that black dialect be used in the teaching of reading (Baratz and Baratz, 1970) or that aspects of black culture be incorporated into the curriculum in order to derive learning tools that are consonant with the previous experience of black children (Hale, 1982). Such writers hold that teachers must be sensitized to cultural differences so that, rather than block learning, familiar experiential patterns can be used to advantage.[8]

The present study, to some extent, offers an alternative explanation. Attempting to coalesce history, culture and learning, Hale recently has suggested using the humanities to create an educational model that will enable educators to understand and facilitate the expressive styles that emerge from black culture. Culture, however, is more than a group's art, music, and movement. It is the patterns of organization that hold diverse people together and the systems of beliefs and meanings to which the group subscribes. Thus, analysis of forms must take place at a deeper level.

The Need for the Study

Though work is now being done which illuminates the clash of cultures that minority children experience in public schooling, little is known about the cultural patterning that children experience before entering school and how or if cultural values are encouraged in settings other than the home. Despite the millions of dollars invested in preschool programs for the 'disadvantaged', quantitative studies have demonstrated conflicting results from which it has been difficult to generalize (Datta, 1979).[9]

Writers from various persuasions have expressed a need for studies of early education that are comparative and contexted in nature.

Discussing the difficulties that arise when children with differing socio-cultural and linguistic orientations enter public school, Bernstein (1971) notes: 'A comparative study of middle-class and working-class nursery schools would be invaluable' (p. 38). Wozniak (1974) indicates that, with the exception of Skinner's reinforcement psychology, there has been an 'almost complete alienation of the study of learning in children from the context in which a major share of that learning takes place, namely the school' (p. 69). And Mead (1971), in relating early childhood to later education, insists that 'What we need is more basic research, on the one hand, and more devices for assaying the quality of pre-school experience on the other' (p. 76). Yet, as late as 1979, Zimmer writes that 'There has been little qualitative research done by sociologists and anthropologists on informal child-care arrangements.' And he reiterates the need for 'comparative ethnographies of different types of centers' (p. 139).

The Study

The present study was launched in the fall of 1980 when I began observations in two early education classrooms. The study was inductive, and the categories and formal devices presented in the chapters that will comprise the body of the study were devised over time, both to stabilize the flux of movement and activity and to clarify observable differences. After the analysis was more or less complete (late in 1981), I began the arduous task of determining how my data meshed with other work in the field.

I surveyed a formidable literature on cross-cultural child rearing practices and came to realize that the patterns that I had observed and chronicled had been noted by other researchers, working in various cultural settings. To my knowledge, this literature has never been utilized to help to understand the processes by which children learn in early education environments within the United States. It is this work, then, which is summarized in the review of literature which follows.

After a chapter on ethnographic method, the study details how different patterns are constructed in the respective settings, and different child rearing practices are seen as different means of reaching different ends. Time, space and activity are shown to be frames for organizing meaningful social interaction, serving as powerful analytic devices for demonstrating and understanding the reticulated nature of cultural patterning.

Notes

1 In his preface to *Genetics and Education* (1972) Jensen explains that his interest in quantitative genetics arose out of his survey of the literature on cultural deprivation and his realization that genetic factors were almost totally neglected. The public outcry and professional condemnation of his work have been unmatched since Darwin's time. Here he gives a vivid description of the events which preceded and followed the publication of his views.

2 One Congressman read the entire 163-page article into the Congressional Record so that separatists could refer to it as social and scientific fact (Edson, 1969).

3 Here the term 'environmental' refers specifically to theories which were premised on the belief that lower class children were not provided adequate cognitive stimulation early in life. This specific use of the term does not include prenatal care (maternal malnutrition and trauma), premature birth, or the nutritional or physiological care of the infant. These issues are beyond the scope of this paper.

4 Though frequently operating with parental support, Project Head Start likewise has removed children from their homes under the presumption that they are 'behind.' Head Start was begun in 1965 as an early education intervention program to enable 'disadvantaged' children to compensate for cultural deficits in order to achieve later school success. The project enrolled 560,000 children during the first summer alone (Gordon and Wilkerson, 1966, p. 31). Head Start was intended to improve physical well-being and to provide social and psychological services, as well as to improve intellectual ability and academic performance (McDavid *et al*, 1967). Begun as an eight-week pilot program, it was soon expanded to one year. However, by the end of the decade the War on Poverty and its component divisions (the Elementary and Secondary Education Act of 1965, training programs such as Job Corps and the Neighborhood Youth Corps, and adult programs heralding under the Manpower Development and Training Act of 1962), had failed by most indices in their attempts to equalize social and economic differences (Cicierelli *et al*, 1969; Carnoy and Levin, 1975). Test scores did not improve or were not maintained; segregation increased, and, despite massive expenditures, schools themselves, both urban and rural, did not seem appreciably to improve.

The major literature on Head Start has focused on aggregating data on individual children (Datta, 1979) or on variations in programming (length of time in the program, length of the program, age at onset of the program, etc.) (Palmer and Anderson, 1979). Evidence that dramatic initial successes faded after a year or two (for example, Westinghouse, 1969) generally has been interpreted as a need for more long-term and comprehensive services (Richmond, Stipek and Zigler, 1979). Though the emphasis has changed in recent years from raising IQs to encouraging 'social competence' (Zigler, Valentine and Seitz, 1979; Zigler and Seitz, 1980), the fundamental asssumption that individual children need to change (i.e., that they 'lack' competence) has not changed.

5 The 'culturally disadvantaged' were presumed to be the poor, especially minorities such as Blacks, Mexican-Americans, Puerto Ricans, and American Indians. Bernstein (1961) more generally defined cultural deprivation as a deficiency of language. Hess and Shipman (1965) spoke of a deficiency of meaning, and Caldwell (1967) defined it as a 'deprived environment'.

The argument went as follows: children from the lower classes (and this includes many minority children) too often grow up in an environment defined by unemployment, welfare, poor diet and ill health. These are problems which leave children's beleaguered parents with little time to attend to their basic needs, let alone encourage them to converse or to provide them with anything more stimulating than a sustenance existence. Children thus enter school language-deprived, and, due to cumulative deficiencies, experience progressive retardation throughout their school years.

6 In extensive studies in California, for example, Mercer and Brown (1973) found four times more Mexican Americans and three times more Blacks labeled 'mentally retarded' because of their performance on standardized tests than would be expected from their percentage in the population at large. Yet in 1973 all of the major IQ tests used in the United States had been standardized on a Caucasian population. The Stanford-Binet, the Wechsler Intelligence Scale for Children, the Peabody Picture Vocabulary Test and the Standard Progressive Matrices all excluded Black, Indian and Mexican-American children from the standardization samples. Though these children would seem to be outside the population parameters as defined by the test designers, it has been these same tests which have been used to place minority children in classes for the mentally retarded. LeVine (1970) among others, has noted in such testing that fundamental premises of inferential statistics frequently have been by-passed, questions regarded sampling bias, response sets (fear of 'foreign' investigators, acquiescence in strange situations, etc.), and differential familiarity with testing or with the investigator as a type of person.

7 A simple example serves to clarify how context can play a major role in the determination of how a child develops. It has been argued that the radical change in sleep/wake behavior noted in American infants during the first year is an index of the physiological maturation of the brain. However, differences in sleep patterns between American and African babies can more readily be explained by the different contexts in which the babies live. In white America babies usually sleep in their own beds and are often alone in a room. Parents are eager to have their babies 'sleep through the night' and so encourage this behavior at every opportunity. In rural Africa, by contrast, infants are constantly with others whose activity influences their opportuni-

ties for sleep. At night babies sleep with their mothers and may wake throughout the night to nurse (Harkness, 1980).

8 The problem of what diverse people (staff, parents, etc.) think children should learn (and what they do learn) can be nonethelesss complex and frequently contradictory (Joffe, 1977; Zimmer, 1979).

9 Intervention studies were devised as deliberately different treatments. Geographic locations varied, and programs differed according to type, amount (12–30 hours per week), duration, and according to the age at which treatment was effected. Both theory and practice varied from program to program. And dependent variables — indices of 'success' — ranged from the percentage of children retained in grade or relegated to special education classes to scores on reading achievement tests, arithmetic achievement tests and IQ tests to some measure of the degree of parental participation and support (Palmer and Anderson, 1979). Attempts to synthesize such diverse efforts raise questions that cannot easily be dismissed. For example, reviewers frequently use categorical distinctions such as 'center-based' vs. 'home-based' in order to make more general statements about the effectiveness of one type of program relative to another. However, home-based programs (for example, Gordon) typically were established for infants, whereas center-based or home/center programs were more common for two 1/2–5 year olds (for example, Karnes and Levenstein). Such confounding of variables makes it all the more difficult to tease out factors of relevance. Further complicating the issue is the fact that, even when different studies ostensibly use the same measure of academic achievement, results are mixed:

> Gordon (WISC-R at age 10; personal communication), Beller (Standford-Binet SB at 10, 1979), Gray (Stanford-Binet at 10; Gray and Klaus, 1970), and Palmer (WISC-R at 12, 1976a) report statistically significant differences on IQ between experimental and control children, with the differences on IQ between experimental and control children, with the former averaging about 8 IQ points more than the controls. Seitz (Abelson, Zigler and DeBlasi, 1974) report significant differences on the Peabody Picture Vocabulary Test (PPVT) between nine-year-olds formerly in a Head Start-Follow Through program and their controls.
>
> Deutsch (SB at 9; Deutsch, Taleporos, and Victor) reports no significant differences between experimental and control children, although differences did exist at age 6. Weikart (WISC at 14; Schweinhart and Weikart, 1977) found no differences, nor did Miller at age 8 (Miller and Dyer) or age 13 (Miller, personal communication) when her four experimental groups were compared with the controls on the SB and the WISC-R (*Ibid*, p. 455).

In the attempt to 'show significance' fudging is not uncommon; thus results frequently 'approach significance' or otherwise indicate that change is in a positive direction (p < 10). Even the most recent assessments cannot definitely credit such programs with the reduction in White-Black differences that have been noted in some achievement areas. And the U.S. Commission on Civil Rights (1978) has shown that, while earning differentials have decreased between Whites and Blacks, differential unemployment and differential poverty rates have increased (Burton and Jones, 1982).

2 *Related Literature*

For every child early in life when the first thought hovers and begins to take form, others are there to guide its formation, and, when expressed, to value or to dismiss it. Adults and older children help the young child to learn the rules of group membership: who will help, what is important, how to be, why some things are done and not others. This complex process is the means by which a human infant becomes a member of a human group and the means by which distinct groups (for example tribes, sub-cultures and social classes) are reproduced and perpetuated.

Enculturation entails learning one's place within the group, learning one's rights and responsibilities; it is the process of learning the whole complex of meanings that defines the social reality of the group and the rules which allow a newcomer to function within it.

Much of the educational research literature that has influenced social policy has been formulated under the assumption that minority adults are inexperienced or inept parents and that children therefore are deprived of adequate stimulation. Cross-cultural studies of child rearing suggest instead that throughout the world cultural groups make meaningful adaptations to environments that are strikingly different and that an accurate understanding of child rearing practices must take context into account.

The present chapter is organized around a presentation of several issues regarding cultures and child rearing:

(i) culture as a meaningful system of beliefs and practices;
(ii) variability across cultures in patterns of child rearing, linking practices to the contexts, in which people live; and
(iii) a discussion of how cultural groups have been defined.

The first section outlines major theoretical perspectives which address questions regarding the perpetuation and alternation of social organizations. The symbolic interactionist perspective is defined as a means by which researchers have studied how individuals construct meaningful patterns through interaction with others.

The second section reviews studies which deal with the external conditions which influence child rearers and the meaningful adaptations made by child rearers to these conditions. Both cross-cultural (idiographic and comparative) studies and social class studies of child-rearing within complex societies are reviewed. The comparative studies especially depict child rearing practices as strongly influenced by social and economic conditions.

The third section outlines ways in which numerous researchers have attempted to define cultural differences. It addresses questions of how these adaptations are conveyed to children and the behaviors children manifest as a consequence. The subsection on the macroanalysis of cultural differences is concerned with the first of these questions, suggesting broad differences which, as Greenfield and Bruner (1969) have noted, are deeply rooted in systems of socialization. The second subsection is concerned with the question of what behaviors are manifest as a consequence of different child rearing practices. Since within-group personality and cognitive differences are a major means by which cultural differences are defined, two major developmental theories that have influenced early education are briefly reviewed: the personality theory of Freud and the cognitive developmental theory of Piaget. Studies are cited which question whether there is a universal pattern of development. Numerous researchers hold that development is related to context and that a situational theory of child development is needed to account for cross-cultural differences.

The third subsection, that on the microanalysis of differences, deals with the question of child behaviors by reviewing studies which define more specifically the nature of cultural differences in verbal orientation and in non-verbal communication, for example, 'syncing' responses while speaking and apparent differences in attention-getting behavior. The differing utilizations of time, space and activity speak to the issue of what adults *do* in context that may have an effect on the subsequent behavior of children.

Culture as a Meaningful System of Beliefs and Practices[1]

How human groups are maintained and organized, questions of the nature of the social order, have been central to the study of both sociology and anthropology. Durkheim described abstract structures which created patterns of solidarity. 'Mechanical solidarity', he suggested, was typical of simple societies that were bound together by common beliefs and practices. Resulting from the collective conscience, justice, retribution, ritual, religion, norms and taboos stemmed from 'a quite mechanical reaction, from movements which are passionate and in great part non-reflective' (Durkheim, 1933, p. 108). 'Organic solidarity', by contrast, was characteristic of complex industrial societies which were highly differentiated, specialized and interdependent. Organic solidarity was expressed by different kinds of relations and by rights which 'do not cause the people whom they put in contact with one another to concur; they do not demand any cooperation; they simply restore and maintain' (*Ibid.*, p. 118).

Durkheim believed that the division of labor would allow for individuality in a social context. For the first time in history individuals performing different functions could be united by their interdependent roles (Nisbet, 1966). Yet in the very development of his argument Durkheim recognized that its extension meant that he would align himself with the utilitarian Herbert Spencer who stressed the fact that individuals would increasingly unite only through restitutive sanctions of contract based on the division of labor. Thus, in the process, he powerfully altered his argument by recognizing that the stability of the second required that it be firmly set in the continuation, in whatever form, of the first (*Ibid.*). Modern society, he would hereafter argue, could not survive so long as individuals remain detached from one another or united only through transitory contractual ties.[2]

Durkheim maintained that societies held together by 'organic solidarity' would forever suffer internal conflict unless they were also united by 'mechanical' beliefs and symbols. And later Lévi-Strauss (1963) made a strong case for the reverse, showing how societies united by 'mechanical solidarity' were also differentiated internally, not by the division of labor, but rather by symbolic distinctions such as 'totemic' classifications.

Durkheim was strongly influenced by the biologists of his time, seeing society as an organic whole that was either 'normal' or 'pathological.' Society, he believed, could be examined by analyzing 'functional' needs, by examining, that is, how the parts served the whole.

Functionalism per se was further refined and developed by two early anthropologists, Bronislaw Malinowski and A.R. Radcliffe-Brown. Malinowski assumed that aspects of culture existed to fulfill human needs, a line of reasoning that has received much criticism in the literature on the grounds that it was implicitly circular. Whether one examines customs, artifacts, rituals, or beliefs, cultural items exist to fulfill needs; if they exist, there must be need for them (Turner, 1967).

Radcliffe-Brown, however, preferred the term 'structuralism' to refer to the organismic study of society. Instead of 'needs' he spoke of 'necessary conditions of existence.' The conditions necessary for any given social group were thus empirical questions. 'In recognizing the diversity of conditions necessary for the survival of different systems, analysis would avoid asserting that every item of a culture must have a function and that items in different cultures must have the same function' (*Ibid*, p. 22).

Structural-functional approaches, however, have been criticized for the way in which they depict people as passive in the light of powerful structural forces. By contrast, Weber saw meaning expressed in the intentional actions of individuals. People were not done to but were the doers of social action.[3]

The study of social processes from the symbolic interactionist perspective is a conceptual reversal of structural approaches. Focusing on micro, rather than macro, structures, symbolic interactionists have sought to study how social processes originate and are maintained through individuals in meaningful interaction with others. Rather than being pawns of psychological or social structures individuals are perceived as actively *constructing* meaningful patterns of action.

George Herbert Mead (1934) was the first to interlink mind, self, and society in a coherent approach to interaction. According to Mead, the human mind was constituted by its use of symbols and by the ability to mentally evaluate alternative courses of action. Mind was thus a process rather than a pre-formed structure. Mind emerged from the selectivity inherent in the socialization process. Through this process the infant came to share 'common meanings' with others. As the child learned to understand and use these 'conventional gestures' he or she learned also 'to take the role of the other' (i.e., to interpret the other's needs, wants and actions), thereby learning how to cooperate with others.

From these capabilities a sense of self likewise emerged, the ability to see oneself as an object in interaction. Through the achievement of a 'self conception,' actions became consistent. As the self developed, the individual became capable of taking the role of the 'generalized other,' of comprehending and integrating the beliefs, attitudes and norms of a broad 'community of attitudes.'

Society, then, was seen to represent patterned interactions among diverse individuals. Unlike structuralist approaches, seeing 'mind' as the genesis of society enabled the analyst to account for social change. Through constant role-taking, evaluating and interacting the individual both maintained and changed as new alternatives came to light.

As disciple and interpreter of Mead, Blumer (1967) elaborated and labeled the symbolic interactionist perspective. For Blumer, individuals acted meaningfully and with intention and worked cooperatively with others to construct symbolic patterns of interaction and actual structures and objects. While much of interaction was patterned and repetitive, individuals were capable of changing their actions in response to changes in the environment. The nature of social organization could best be understood, therefore, by focusing on the symbolic processes by which individuals 'made meaning' with one another.

The relative efficacy of the structural-functional approach *vs.* the symbolic interactionist approach has been a topic of ongoing debate within the social sciences. Nonetheless, understanding how systems provide order and how people create meaningful systems are central to the study of culture.[4] In the section that follows, the discussion focuses on the content of cultural studies of child rearing, irrespective of the theory that informs individual studies.

Variability Across Cultures in Patterns of Child Rearing

There is already a wealth of anthropological literature which indicates extraordinary variability across cultures in systems of child rearing. Yet anthropologists have differed among themselves in the extent to which they have focused on unique or common features when making comparisons across groups. This section is particularly concerned with studies which have dealt with the external conditions which influence child rearers and the adaptations made to these conditions. Early anthropologists assumed that culture itself was universal and that ostensible differences were evolutionary and in degree, as in the development of the technology of cloth (Tylor, 1904). Around the world children are able to suck, chew, drink, eat, flex, grasp, crawl and toddle, walk, talk, sleep, laugh, cry, and learn — through complex processes only partially understood — to relate to others.

Yet others believed that it was because of the similarities that it was possible to compare. Since comparison across groups was a form of meta-analysis, differences were seen in bold relief against a background that was shared. Thus, Benedict (1934) defined culture in particular rather than in universal terms. Culture was that which defined the group, the roles, rituals, beliefs, and practices that unite a single group and make groups distinct one from another. Through the 'enculturation process' groups and group differences were believed to be perpetuated. Child training and culture were thus interlocked. As LeVine (1970) has written, '. . . in order to know *how* a culture affects the development of behavior dispositions in a child, one has to know about the culture as well as about the child' (p. 560).

Idiographic Studies of Child Rearing

Mead herself initially believed that there were commonalities across cultures and that through what she called the 'cross-cultural control method' researchers could test developmental hypotheses by comparing children from cultures that differed in significant ways. Though comparisons were to be done in naturalistic settings, variations between groups could be considered as variations in independent variables (Sears, 1975). After her fieldwork in Bali, however, and after inspecting the famous Bateson photographs that revealed the extensiveness of behavioral, postural, and gestural differences, Mead rejected her original assumption and came to believe that each culture was unique (Mead, 1946).

Mead went on to study the relation between child development and culture. Like Benedict, she adopted the position that culture was patterned and integrated, differing in many ways from other cultural systems, not simply in one or two strikingly apparent ways. Mead proceeded to chronicle extraordinary variation in systems of rearing and educating children (for example Mead 1959/76; Mead and Wolfenstein, 1955).

In the 1940s and 1950s major studies depicted patterns of child-rearing in widely different societies. In his study of 'the Hopi child' Dennis described the intimate relation between child-rearing practices and child behavior, contending that 'the anthropological description of child care is inevitably more complete than is the psychological account of child behavior' (Dennis, 1940, p. vi). Interestingly, though Dennis described extensive cultural differences between Hopi and white child rearing practices during the first year (the Hopi use of a cradleboard, breast feeding, demand feeding, late weaning, etc.) he found no real difference in age of onset of walking and no observable difference in behavior between children of the two cultures at the end of the first year.[5]

DuBois (1944) in her study of the people of Alor, took as her basic premise Kardiner's (1939) assumption that primary institutions, in particular child training practices, produce a basic structure for personality, which, in turn, influences the secondary institutions of the culture. Believing that a psychological orientation was necessary to the understanding of social processes, DuBois described the processes of child training from infancy through early childhood, late childhood, adolescence, and adulthood and provided in-depth autobiographies of eight Alor individuals. By tracing the repeated experiences, relationships and values which occurred and reoccurred throughout the individual's life, she believed that it would be possible, not only to gauge variations, but also central tendencies.

DuBois depicted a society in which anxiety and distrust were common manifestations of interpersonal relationships. Since mothers were responsible for the agricultural fields, infants were left to the care of appointed nurses or older siblings from an early age. The society did not reward mothering, and, since, according to DuBois, women felt cheated in infancy, mothers in turn teased and cheated their children. The result was that the male child found his future relations with women tenuous at best, while the female forever, and to no avail, searched for a male-female relationship that would provide her with the loving mother she never had. The mutual distrust that was generated was the foundation of continuous infidelity, repeated divorces, frequent abortions and resentment at bearing and rearing children. Marriages were held together by complex financial arrangements which acted as a stay against chaos. Since most adults experienced a lack of control in childhood, in adulthood there was a quest for control of others, for the women through the withdrawal of food, for the men through the managements of finances. The financial system itself was used, according to Kardiner, 'to channelize the enormous amount of intrasocial hostility' (Kardiner in DuBois, 1944, p. 189).

In a later and classic treatise on childhood and society Erikson (1950/63) explored the interrelation between three principles of organization: somatic, ego, and societal. According to Erikson, processes inherent in the organism have traditionally been the domain of biology, the organization of experience the domain of psychology, and the social organization of groups of geographical and historical significance the domain of the social sciences. He suggested that each had been isolated from the total living situation that gave them meaning and attempted to reintegrate them using the psychoanalytic constructs of ego psychology.

Comparative Studies of Child Rearing

Cross-cultural comparative studies

Mead's belief that cultures could only be studied idiographically and described in isolation was not universally accepted. Isolated studies served as evidence that environmental conditions, child rearing practices and subsequent behavioral effects varied across cultures, but little was known about the nature of the interrelationship or about how varied cultures might also be similar in certain respects.

Some of the most well-known studies, particularly regarding cross-cultural child rearing practices, have been attempts to make meaningful comparisons across groups. Whiting and Child (1953) used quantitative methods for studying groups of children but applied these methods to groups of cultures. Using extant ethnographies of more than seventy different societies they attempted to correlate antecedent and consequent conditions for a wide range of child training factors by looking at how practices around weaning and toilet training had subsequent effect in terms of fixation, guilt, and fear of persons and spirits. Statistical techniques were then used to determine how the two conditions varied together among human groups. Though a number of their predictions about relationships cross-culturally did not bear out, the confirmation of others led them to believe that there were some principles of human development that held across cultures.

Concentrating on child training and projective systems as observable variables, they hypothesized that there was a causal sequence among maintenance systems (the basic economic, social and political systems of a group that allowed for the food, shelter and protection of individuals), child training practices, personality variables, and projective systems. For example, marriage practices, as a form of social structure, appeared to have generalizable effects on consequent child training practices. Whiting and Child found that in systems of sororal polygyny (in which wives are sisters), initial child training is more indulgent and subsequent socialization less severe than in either monogamous or non-sororal polygynous situations.[6]

Since many of the ethnographies used in this comprehensive analysis lacked information about significant variables, Whiting (1963) later organized a team of researchers from Yale, Harvard and Cornell to do in-depth studies of child rearing practices in six widely different cultures. Groups in Kenya, India, Okinawa, Mexico, the Philippines, and New England were studied. Each description was divided into two parts: the ethnographic background, the depiction of the maintenance systems that set the parameters for child training, and child training practices specific to each setting.

The studies focused on issues salient to the researchers at the time: individual and cultural differences in personality, particularly in the areas of aggression, dependency, and the internalization of mechanisms of behavioral control. Field teams were trained both in the issues to be addressed and in the methods of data collection to be utilized. Direct and extensive observation, careful sampling (selected by the home-based research team rather than by the fieldworkers), and attention to variability within groups replaced earlier methods of second-hand reporting and unsubstantiated generalization. Again, the research was focused on hypotheses defining the relationship between specific patterns of child training and subsequent differences in personality.

Based on data gathered by the six field teams of the 'Six Cultures' project, two later studies examined maternal behavior and child behavior. Minturn and Lambert (1964) considered child behavior as an end result and looked for its antecedents in the maternal beliefs, attitudes and practices which were based upon adaptations to specific natural and social environments. Whiting and Whiting (1975) in the last 'Six Cultures' report focused instead on child behavior, looking at the effect child training practices had upon the child.

Based on an interview with mothers similar to that employed by Sears, Maccoby and Levin (1953), Minturn and Lambert used factor analysis to identify factor patterns within each of six societies.[7] Specifically the researchers wanted to know what the mothers *did* to foster certain kinds of behavior in children. These behaviors were then put back into the original context in order to make them understandable in concrete terms. Results of the investigation indicated that living patterns and economic activities accounted for most of the between culture differences on mean factor scores.

> It now appears that the pressures impinging upon the growing child are much more in the nature of by-products of the horde of apparently irrelevant considerations that impinge upon the parents. These considerations of household composition, size of family, work load, etc., determine the time and energy that mothers have available to care for children. They determine the range and context of mother-child relations and the context in which these relations must take place. The coerciveness of these forces becomes apparent in the broad spectrum of cross-cultural comparison. The mother of Orchard Town, alone in her own house and surrounded by neighbors with whom she has no kinship ties; the mother of Khalapur, confined by custom to her courtyard shared by other confined women with whom she has no ties of blood; the mother of Tarong, secure in the village in which she was raised among blood and affilial kinsmen; and the mother of Gusii, supporting her family without her husband's aide and sharing her yard with co-wives whom she may suspect of bewitching her and her children, all face very different

worlds. Each must solve the problems of these worlds and pass
on to her children, both the problems and the solutions (*Ibid.*,
p. 291).

Context, in effect, was seen to play a major role in influencing the child
training practices which, in turn, influenced child behavior.

The factors Minturn and Lambert isolated were different than those
defined by the original research team. They hypothesized that key
factors were maternal warmth, maternal instability, proportion of time
that mothers cared for children, responsibility training and aggression
training, related to both mothers and peers. Two hypotheses appeared
to find support both in the within group analysis of differences in the six
cultures studied and in the cross-cultural analysis using the Human
Relations Area Files. These were: (i) the contention that mothers spent
less time with children when other women were available; and (ii) that
children were more severely punished for fighting when they had to
share close living quarters.

The two hypotheses relating to maternal personality, maternal
warmth and instability, received little support from the HRAF but some
from the individual differences analysis. The researchers suggested that
this may be indicative of the incompleteness of ethnographic material in
this regard. Finally, their hypotheses that responsibility training and
punishment for mother-directed aggression were less severe when
mothers made little or no contribution to the economic resources of the
family remained untested.

In later analysis of the 'Six Cultures' data, Whiting and Whiting
attempted to isolate constellations of factors that influenced certain
forms of social behavior. Two dimensions of behavior evolved, what the
researchers called Dimension A, nurturant-responsible *vs.* dependent-
dominant, and Dimension B, sociable-intimate *vs.* authoritarian-
aggressive. The first dimension consisted of

(offers help plus offers support plus suggests responsibly) minus
(seeks help plus seeks attention plus seeks dominance). The
score for Dimension B consisted of (acts sociably plus assaults
sociably plus touches) minus (reprimands plus assaults) (*op. cit.*,
p. 174).

The six cultures fell into four typologies: Juxtlahuaca (Mexico) and
Tarong (the Philippines) had children who had positive average scores
on both dimensions; Khalapur (India) and Taira (Okinawa) children fell
on the negative side of both dimensions; Nyansongo (Kenya) children
fell on the positive side of Dimension A and the negative side of

Dimension B; and Orchard Town (US) children had scores that fell on the negative side of Dimension A and the positive side of Dimension B.

Significantly, the Whitings related these constellations of personality factors to the context in which the children lived. For example, children who scored high on 'nurturant-responsible' and low on 'dependent-dominant' (Nyansongo, Juxlahuaca, and Tarong) all lived in simple societies with little occupational specialization, a kin-based political structure, no professional priesthood, no public buildings, and no class or caste system. Women worked hard, and children were expected to do chores and care for siblings.

By contrast, Khalapur and Orchard Town, whose children had relatively high scores on egoism and low scores on nurturance, were societies in which there was a highly specialized labor force, a central government, a priesthood, social stratification, and nucleated villages with public buildings. In these societies, women tended to depend on their husbands for support, and a high premium was placed on the children's schooling and achievement.

Dimension B appeared dependent on differences in the structure of households. Orchard Town children who scored high on sociable-intimate and low on authoritarian-aggressive lived in independent nuclear families. The husband and wife ate and slept together; both cared for the children, and the wife was seldom abused. In Nyansongo and Khalapur, however, where children scored high on authoritarian-aggressive and low on sociable-intimate, there was a domestic structure based on the patrilineal extended family. Husbands and wives usually ate at separate times and in separate places and seldom slept in the same bed. Husbands were not expected to help with infants and wife-beating was permitted.

Such evidence lends support to the hypothesis that clusters of personality traits are strongly influenced by social and economic factors. The socialization of children appears, not surprisingly, to conform to adult role requirements.

> Offering help and support is required of adults living in simpler societies, where the meeting of kin-based obligations and reciprocity with neighbors is essential; boasting and egoistic dominance are out of place there. In more complex communities, where relatives and neighbors are seen as competitors rather than persons to be helped and supported, boasting and egoistic dominance are often more appropriate responses than offering help and support ... These values are apparently transmitted to the child before the age of six (*Ibid.*, pp. 178–9).

Though the Whitings had hoped to examine the extent to which these variables had the same effects within and across cultures, there was not sufficient data to test this hypothesis. Their research, however, makes a strong case that differences in learning environments help to generate differences in social behavior.

Social class studies of child rearing within complex societies

Although much research within complex Western societies has depicted lower class or minority child-rearing practices as deficient or inferior, some researchers have attempted, like those doing cross-cultural research, to understand the connections among environment, adult child rearing practices and subsequent behavioral effects on children.

Anthropology and sociology typically portray the enculturation or socialization process as a preparation of the young for specific societal roles. Durkheim (1933) demonstrated early on principles that created a division of labor within complex societies and later showed that education prepared children for specific places within that society (Durkheim, 1954). The way in which social-structural features influence child training, however, has been a topic of only recent interest.

In a widely-quoted review of literature on child training from 1928 to 1957 Bronfenbrenner (1958) demonstrated how early studies focused on mother-child interaction with little reference to the context in which those interactions took place. Social class differences in maternal behavior were clearly defined, with middle-class mothers being more 'democratic,' while lower-class mothers were shown to be more 'authoritarian.' Middle-class mothers used more 'love-oriented' discipline (disapproval, guilt and withdrawal of affection), while lower-class mothers used more physical punishment.

In a more recent review Hess (1970) noted that, since most research has concentrated on the effects of parental behavior upon children, social class differences have been analyzed in terms of class differences in parental behavior without reference to the fact that parents themselves live in different environments. Instead, he asks a series of questions that interrelate the society and its institutions with various conditions of life, adult behavior, and the subsequent training of children:

> What are the *conditions* of the external social and cultural world in which the child lives? What are the *adaptive consequences* which adults in the environment acquire in their interaction with the system? *In what specific forms do these adult orienta-*

tions appear in interaction with children? What are the *be-havioral outcomes* of these experiences in children? (p. 463)

As cited in the introduction, these questions form the cornerstone of the current study.

Several writers have demonstrated that social-structural features help to create lingusitic and behavioral differences within complex societies. In seminal work in Britain Bernstein (1971) suggested that different social classes created different situations, which, in turn, resulted in different situational codes.[8] Strongly influenced by Vygotsky and Luria, Bernstein saw language as an orienting and regulating system. 'Restricted code,' spoken by the lower classes, is highly contextual with meaning being subtly conveyed through gesture, intonation and other non-verbal means and words being more ritualized and predictable. 'Elaborated code,' used by the middle- and upper-classes, is more personal and individualistic; the subtle arrangement of words conveys feeling and the modulation of volume and tone are less important than the words themselves.

Bernstein hypothesized that 'the greater the differentiation of the child's experience, the greater his ability to differentiate and elaborate objects in his environment' (p. 28). Like Vygotsky, he saw the individuation process directly related to the degree of language specificity. Whereas the lower-class individual speaks the language of the group (short commands, simple questions, and statements that are descriptive, tangible and emotive rather than logical), middle-class and upper-class individuals distinguish themselves from others linguistically as well as in fact. Language structure, the way in which words and sentences are related, reflects, according to Bernstein, the very structure of social interaction and orientation to the environment.

Kohn (1959a, 1959b) saw a link among occupations, parental values and child rearing practices. Studying the values and attitudes of over 10,000 families, he found that parents who are restricted in the workplace tend to be more authoritarian with their children, whereas parents who enjoy a good deal of control over their work allow their children more freedom and expression. In such ways, Kohn believed, different child rearing practices reflect an adaptation to different situational variables (see also the subsequent discussion of Rosalie Cohen's work). Bernstein, Kohn and Cohen all suggest that factors of social class strongly influence child rearing practices, that a 'group' orientation seems common to the experience of lower class people, whereas an 'individual' orientation is apparent among the middle and upper-middle classes.[9]

Such research indicates a developing trend away from the study of class differences in parental (child-rearing) behavior toward research which demonstrates the influence of broader social structural factors on child-rearers themselves. Numerous writers are now arguing that development must be understood 'ecologically' (for example, Bronfenbrenner, 1976; Harkness, 1980), while others state more explicitly the need for a 'situational theory of child development' (deLone, 1979).

Studies of How Cultural Differences are Manifest

This section addresses the question of how environmental adaptations are conveyed to children and the question of what behaviors children manifest as a consequence. Anthropological studies that attempt to define cultural difference have focused on various levels of analysis. At the macro level writers have, through cultural comparison, defined broad adaptations which appear to infuse the life of a particular group and strongly influence the individuals within it. At the level of the individual others have observed cultural differences in individual personality and cognitive orientations. Still others have looked at the micro level of interaction in families and in schools.

Macro Analysis of Cultural Difference

Benedict (1934) was perhaps the first to develop the notion that groups of peoples might organize themselves around vastly different principles. She perceived the culture of the Hopi and Zuni tribes as being Apollonian with emphasis on rationality and group cohesion, and she contrasted it with the Dionysian culture of the Plains Indians which stressed personal struggle and individual excellence. Her portraits have since been seriously questioned.

In addressing child rearing practices more directly, Eggan (1956/76) studied affect as a device for teaching and learning among the Hopi. She demonstrated how Hopi children learned to be *interdependent* rather than *independent*, to be schooled in kinship, in sharing and mutual obligation. Living under the constant fear of drought and of starvation, the group depended on cooperation. Since drought, pestilence and death were attributed to 'bad heart,' it was vital that everyone keep a 'good heart.' Children thus learned from an early age that security and well-being lay in group solidarity rather than in individual distinction.

Greenfield and Bruner have suggested that cultural value systems (collective *vs.* individualistic) have deep roots in systems of socialization. Whereas the former orientation is characteristic of tradition-bound cultures, the latter seems representative of societies that are progress-oriented. Greenfield and Bruner believe that a collective orientation develops where individuals lack power over the physical world. In naturalistic observations of the Wolof in Africa it was discovered that children lacked manipulatory experience and that socialization focused on social relations rather than natural phenomena. Bruner concludes: 'This complex, moreover, is held to be found in all African societies and to stem from common cultural features' (Greenfield and Bruner, 1969, p. 642). More recently, working from a different body of knowledge and from different experience, Hall is seemingly awed by a similar discovery: 'it had not occurred to me until recently, while working on a theory of identification, that the world of man divides into cultures whose members cut the apron strings and those whose members do not' (Hall, 1976, p. 199).

Though Western industrialized nations are generally considered prototypes of societies in which individuals are socialized to be independent and achieving, not all groups within the society have experienced the same opportunity. In seminal fieldwork in which she lived for three years with chronically poor black women in an urban American ghetto, Stack (1975) found the word 'kinship' to most accurately describe the interconnectedness of people who must rely on others for their daily survival. Problems, children and resources were shared, and a 'group' focus dominated the daily life of individuals. Most time was spent in the company of other women who shared resources and responsibilities. And, in cramped quarters, an adult would frequently protect her private space from the encroachment of children.

In common parlance black Americans frequently refer to one another as 'kinfolk'. Staples (1974) has noted also the parakinship ties evident in the use of terms such as 'sister,' 'brother,' 'cousin,' and 'bloodbrother' to express closeness where no ties of blood exist.

Nobles (1974) has related the kinship bonds observable in contemporary black communities to the African heritage. According to Nobles, two guiding principles define the African experience: survival of the tribe and the oneness of being. These, coupled with a strong tradition of cooperation and collective responsibility, explain the sense of kinship that has been maintained in the experience of Afro-Americans:

Is not the practice of 'ain't none of my children no better than the others' an expression of the oneness of being, and is not the practice of informal adoptions, 'one more child ain't gonna make no difference' ... expression of survival of the tribe and collective responsibility? (p. 10)[10]

Ramirez and Price-Williams (1976) looked at achievement motivation among different ethnic groups: Anglos, Blacks, and Mexican-Americans. The investigators were interested in determining whether children were motivated to please their families or were motivated by a personal need to achieve. They found Mexican-American and Black children to score higher on family achievement and Anglo males to score higher on self achievement. Interestingly, the females in all three groups had higher scores on family motivation. The findings were summarized by stating that 'contextual conditions are most important in expression of achievement motivation and that the particular form in which achievement is expressed is determined by the definition that culture gives to it' (p. 49). In her study of black migrant workers Lein (1975) expressed this same idea somewhat differently:

> At work, at church, and at home, success is valued by migrants, but competitive success is not as important as general participation. The church, the extended family organization of the migrant camp, and the family organization of the work crew all emphasize cooperation rather than competition (p. 3).

Cultural Differences in Personality and Cognitive Orientations

This section deals specifically with the question of what behaviors are manifest as a consequence of different environments and differing child rearing practices. Theories of development generally hold that there are universal developmental patterns. Such theories have served to depict non-Western and minority children as deficient or retarded in some respects. For example, both within industrialized societies and on a world-wide scale researchers employing Piagetian protocols as indices of cognitive development have demonstrated a developmental 'lag' with minority and non-Western populations (Flavell, 1963; Bruner *et al*, 1966; Dasen, 1972).[11]

Some writers state that cross-cultural differences do not significantly jeopardize the supposed universality of developmental stages (for example, Glick, 1975). Others see development situationally and believe that an accurate understanding of behavior must take context into account. Two major developmental theories are reviewed, and studies which question the universality of these theories are cited. Such distinctions are important because of the value implications inherent in hierarchical theories of development. Where abstraction is perceived as superior to concrete experience, Western middle-class children will invariably be seen as 'superior.' An important issue, however, is whether formal abstraction is at the pinnacle of cognitive development or if instead it is a type of thinking which reflects an adaptation to an environment in which both language and work are detached from concrete experience (see, for example, Buck-Morss, 1975).

Developmental psychology[12]

The major Western psychological theories of the century have focused on individuals and have been premised on a developmental framework. Though Piaget (1950, 1952 and 1970), Freud (1920/53), Kohlberg (1969), Jensen (1973), Erikson (1950/63) and Gagné (1968) have used different terms and, obviously, emphasized different cognitive and personality traits, their theories have certain fundamental commonalities. First, each has been founded on the assumption that there is an ordered progression of change (i.e. development) that characterizes normal human growth. Second, each has presumed this order to be invariant, assuming that failure to go through the series of stages is an indication of arrested development. This linear conception thus has made terms such as 'deprivation' and 'retardation' meaningful. Thirdly, each has presumed that a general theory of — cognitive, psychosocial, moral — development was possible.

That individuals 'develop' would appear to be indisputable. Born with control of few reflexes, human infants gain control gradually. In a matter of months children learn to sit, to crawl, to walk, and to talk, growing ever taller and more capable. As the years progress, most master complex social interactions outside the family and gain skills and knowledge needed for adult participation in a wider society.

Social theorists have assumed that, like physical development, the growth of emotions and thinking is likewise characterized by sequential ordered change. Yet a major question today is whether there is a universal mode of development or to what extent development is context-bound. Though a thorough recapitulation of Western developmental theories is beyond the scope of this paper, two such theories will be briefly reviewed because of the extraordinary scope of their influence: the personality theory of Freud and the cognitive developmental theory of Piaget.

Personality development[13]
Freud broached a theory of development that states that the individual

lives through a sequence of emotional stages during childhood and adolescence. Interaction between the individual and his environment created conflicts which had to be resolved for development to continue.

As a therapist for neurotic adult patients, Freud came to believe that unresolved conflicts during childhood were in large part responsible for adult psychopathology. His theory presupposed that the human infant was driven (motivated) by the pleasure principle, a need to achieve gratification of all impulses. These urges, which Freud called the 'libido,' assumed importance in different forms during different stages of development. The child interacted with the environment in ways that would meet or interfere with the achievement of gratification. Interaction at each stage determined whether the child would pass through the stage successfully or become fixated at the stage, resulting, according to the theory, in later personality disorder.

Begun as a theory of psychopathology, psychoanalytic theory has treated normal development as the transformation of irrational processes into rational ones through the maturation of psychosexual functions (Langer, 1969). Freud and his followers posited five stages of development:

Oral	Birth to 1½
Anal	to 4 years
Phallic	to 6 years
(Oedipal)	
Latency	to adolescence
Genital	adolescence onward

He suggested that these stages were universal. According to the theory, maturation determined the area in which libidinal energy would be invested; therefore, development was seen to be epigenetic in nature. Although stages did not 'grow out of' one another, Freud seems to have suggested that some integration of aspects of earlier stages was necessary to the organized personality.

Cognitive developmental theory[14]
Piaget has been by far the most influential cognitive developmental theorist of the century. Because he saw development as 'universal,' it was not necessary to study large samples of children; only one would demonstrate the entire developmental sequence.

Strongly influenced by biology, Piaget held that the human organism was inherently adaptive, intelligent and the source rather than the recipient of acts (Piaget, 1970). By its nature the human organism interacted with and adapted to the environment. Intelligence was an adaptive mechanism. All species inherited two fundamental tendencies, called 'invariant functions,' adaptation and organization. Adaptation involved two processes, assimilation and accommodation, that occurred simultaneously.

Through the two-fold process of assimilation-accommodation, the structures of the mind developed from a narrow sphere of reflexes to the broad and encompassing 'structures of the whole' of formal operations (Flavell, 1963; Brainerd, 1978). The famous protocols of conservation of quantity, length, area, number, etc. were intended to elucidate the structure of the mind at any point in time.

Unlike the quantifiable continuous model of behaviorism, the qualitative discontinuous model of Piaget has assumed a kind of hierarchic integration (Overton and Reese, 1973). Piaget believed that children's thinking was characterized by four stages or organizations; the child constructed each in turn:

the sensorimotor stage,
the stage of preoperations,
the stage of concrete operations, and
the stage of formal operations.

The end point toward which development and change move was 'equilibration,' which, for Piaget, occurred at about age twelve when formal operational thinking was accomplished. In all the process was characterized by a movement from the simple to the complex, from the concrete to the abstract, and from the absolute to the relative.

Studies which question the universality of developmental stages

Studies of personality development
In numerous cross-cultural studies anthropologists have questioned the 'universality' of Western developmental theories. Though Freud's theory of psycho-social development gave form to processes formerly considered incomprehensible, anthropologists have questioned whether the developmental stages which he proposed are present in all cultures. Malinowski (1927) was the first to cast doubt on the generality of the Oedipal complex by depicting a matrilineal culture in which a boy was under the authority of his uncle rather than his father. In this instance the mother's lover and the boy's dominant role model were two different people. Malinowski argued that the Oedipal complex as conceived by Freud simply did not exist among the Trobriand Islanders.[15]

Even within Western society researchers have shown that personality development appears to be strongly influenced by cultural factors. Kagan and Moss (1962) found that, though many personality characteristics exhibited by children six to ten years of age appeared to be moderately good predictors of adult-related behaviors, others were shown to be modified as the individual adapted to the culture. Passive and dependent behavior in childhood was a good predictor variable for women but not for men. Similarly, aggression was a strong predictor for men but not for women, who tended in adulthood to find substitutes in more socially acceptable behavior: intellectual competitiveness, masculine interests or dependency conflicts. Cultural norms thus appeared to reinforce or to restrain individual personality characteristics.

Studies of cognitive development

Anthropology has also questioned the universality of cognitive developmental stages. Anthropologists have long wondered about the relationship between context and thought (Boas, 1938; Mead, 1946; Whorf, 1956). Most work, however, has been concerned with the product of thought rather than with its processes, assuming that language and thought are synonymous. Major studies have focused upon language per se, the extensiveness of vocabulary and upon systems of categorization (for example, Lévi-Strauss, 1962; Frake, 1961/73). But, as Greenfield and Bruner (1969) point out, this is like studying the growth of logic in children by looking at a logic book. Such procedures tells us little about how thought evolves or how it functions in novel situations. For this reason, Gladwin (1964/73) states that what is most needed are ethnographies that demonstrate how people *learn to think* in specific contexts.

Researchers working in non-Western contexts have suggested that thinking is adaptive to specific settings. Cole and Gay (1972/76) in their work with the Kpelle in Africa have reported that people appear to operate differently on content as a result of training specific to certain environments. Not only did the Kpelle organize information differently (using categories of town things/forest things rather than the more typical Western dichotomy of animate/inanimate), they also displayed a quite different pattern of recall of items to be memorized than did their American counterparts. In earlier work (Gay and Cole, 1967) they demonstrated that the Kpelle could judge the number of cups of rice in a bowl more accurately than Americans but that Americans proved better at sorting cards into three categories according to symbols.

Cole and his colleagues (1971) found differences in responses between Kpelle and American children to be indicative of different cognitive styles. When asked 'logical' questions, such as 'Flumo and Yakpalo always drink cane juice together. Flumo is drinking cane juice. Is Yakpalo drinking cane juice?' traditional Kpelles invariably gave 'wrong' responses. Basing their response on context rather than abstracting from the situation, they typically responded 'Flumo and Yakpalo drink cane juice together ... Yakpalo was not there on that day,' or 'But I was not there. How can I answer such a question?' (Cole *et al*, 1971, p. 187). Cole noted that this did not indicate that Kpelles were incapable of logic. When Kpelles had four or more years of Western schooling, they responded in terms of Western thinking, and, in more familiar situations, such as sorting leaves or measuring rice, they surpassed American subjects. Cole thus hypothesized that specific cognitive orientations and abilities lie more in the *situation* or context than in the cultural group.

Cole's suggestion that thinking is intimately bound to context — so that abstract categories for organizing information are situation-bound — is supported by Gladwin (1970) who attempted to link 'the ghettos and shacks of America with a jewel-like island in the Pacific'. Believing that policy-makers and educators lacked any clear notion of how thinking differed between people who were poor and those not, Gladwin studied 'thinking' in a remote culture, one in which he could not know the 'right' answers ahead of time. He chose to study the art and science of navigation on a small island in Micronesia called Puluwat Atoll. What Gladwin discovered was a system of thought that was complex, inherently consistent, and almost totally non-European in origin. He also found that the two systems were not easily interchangeable. For example, he was puzzled that, though sailing canoes carried compasses as a matter of course, they were seldom used. Once he re-constructed the Puluwat star courses, however, he realized that a simple conversion to compass courses would be problematic. The entire inventory of star courses would have to be modified, and the system of star directions would become asymmetrical.

Gladwin refutes an earlier hypothesis that Trukese navigators lacked an overall (deductive) schema and simply responded minute by minute to the slapping of waves, the strength of the wind, the depth of the boat, and to the stars (see Gladwin, 1964/73). He found this view too simple. Both Western and Puluwat navigators had to think both concretely — and abstractly — in order to navigate the seas. What he suggests is that Western intelligence tests mistake abstraction for something else, what he calls 'heuristics'. Unlike the plans-that-will-work of the Puluwat navigator, heuristics are experimental in nature; they are plans that *might* work. This element of possibility seems related to what Piaget calls 'formal operations'. According to Bruner (1969) formal operations make reality a subset of the possible. What is not known is whether this mode of thinking is universal or is itself an adaptive response to change in a progress-oriented society.

That cognitive development progresses toward formal abstraction in all cultures has been questioned by Bruner (1969) who compared Wolof unschooled, rural children, bush children, and urban schooled children in Africa. Based on this research, Bruner declared that the 'universal' period of egocentrism posited by Piaget may not be so. Children in certain collectively-organized cultures *never* moved from an absolute to a relativist perspective. Such a transition seems culture specific. Bruner and his colleagues found that the rural unschooled children lacked Western self-consciousness. If the children were asked, 'Why do you say that this glass has more water than this one?' they would sit in uncomprehending silence. But if the question was rephrased to 'Why is ... true?' children answered it easily. Bruner concluded that these children did not distinguish between their own thought and the thing itself. Similarly, he expected that they would not comprehend the Western relativistic concept that there might be various points of view regarding a matter. This hypothesis was further supported in later concept formation studies in which these children were unable to categorize according to more than one attribute.[16]

In American studies Cohen (1969/76) has isolated two types of cognitive styles (not suggesting that there are only two): the 'analytic' and the 'relational.' The analytic mode is formal, abstracting and parts-specific. The relational style requires a descriptive mode of abstraction and is self-centered in its orientation to reality; only the global characteristics of a stimulus have meaning, and only in reference to a total context (Cohen, 1967; Kagan, Moss, and Sigel, 1963).

She found the analytic mode characteristic of children reared in formal primary groups such as the middle-class nuclear family and the relational mode typical of children reared in shared function environments. Both were independent of native ability, yet both American schooling — and so-called 'intelligence' tests — were based on the analytic mode. The middle-class orientation of the school and of intelligence tests in general have three major requirements: (i) breadth and depth of general information; (ii) analytic abstraction; and (iii) field articulation (the ability to extract salient information from an embedding context, as in reading comprehension). These skills require a certain approach to organizing and selecting information. As Cohen (1969–76) writes:

Some individuals are 'splitters,' and others are 'lumpers.' Some individuals think attributes of a stimulus have significance in themselves; others think they have significance only in reference to some total context (Kagan, Moss and Sigel, 1963). But the school requires one specific approach to cognitive organization — analytic — so the ability to use it well becomes more critical at higher grade levels (pp. 291–2). (See also the discussion of time and space that follows.)

In short, the cognitive orientation that a child develops appears to be influenced by factors of culture and social class.

Microanalysis of Cultural Difference

Cultures have been characterized in gross terms and between-group differences have been noted both in terms of personality and cognitive orientations. Yet other research has focused on how interactional patterns vary across groups and across situations and on the way in which the macro structure is reproduced at the micro level of interaction in families and in schools. The following studies of verbal and non-verbal interaction are yet another way in which the issue of behavioral differences among children of different cultural groups has been addressed. The subsection on the organization of time, space and activity looks more closely at ways in which adults seem to organize a way of life that, in turn, has subsequent effect on children.

Studies of verbal interaction

Since many minority children have been characterized as ill-prepared for the 'culture of reference' (Burnett, 1969) of the school, recent work has looked at how children behave in different settings. Videotaping minority children in homes, public school classrooms with an without teachers, on playgrounds, etc., Erickson, Florio and Breme (1975) found dramatic interactional differences. A child who seemed quiet, inarticulate and inept with a teacher frequently would appear to be talkative and witty at home. Labov (1972) likewise has demonstrated how black children who fail to demonstrate abilities in school settings will exhibit them in natural settings. And Lein (1975) in her study of speech among black migrant families found children to use their most complex speech patterns with peers, and their simplest speech in the classroom.

More recently, Heath has analyzed differences in the language used in schools and that used in lower-class black (Trackton) homes. At home she found that black children were not regarded as information givers nor as conversational equals to adults, but they nonetheless participated actively in richly diversified verbal interaction. At school, however, teachers were shown to pull topics out of context in their questioning, and, since Trackton parents did not ask their children these kinds of questions, the children themselves had learned different situational responses. Teachers would complain: 'They don't seem able to answer even the simplest questions,' while parents reported, 'My kid, he too scared to talk, 'cause nobody play by the rules he know. At home I can't shut 'im up' (Heath, 1982, p. 107).

Studies of non-verbal communication

Since Birdwhistell's (1952) pioneering work in kinesics, numerous researchers have studied body movement as a form of non-verbal communication.[17] Condon and Sander (1974) found that, between adults and neonates, body movements were isomorphic to the structure of speech. Moreover, newborns synchronized their movements to speech regardless of the language (i.e., American infants 'synced' to Chinese as well as they did to English). They also discovered that two people conversing while wired to electroencephalographs would show such a comparability in brain waves that it seemed as though their nervous systems drove each other. Yet similar studies with black subjects displayed a totally different pattern, suggesting that, while neonates will sync with any language, individuals over time become acculturated to distinct cultural rhythms.

Apparently studying the ramifications of such differences, Byers and Byers (1972) analyzed a thirty-minute segment from a videotape in which a white teacher taught a small group of black and white nursery school students. During this time a white student was able to get the teacher's attention in eight of fourteen attempts; a black student made thirty-five attempts and was successful only four times. Repeated analysis indicated that the black student was out of sync with the teacher's scanning behavior, much more frequently attempting to get the teacher's attention when she was speaking with another student or looking away. The white student typically waited to see the teacher look around the group, then caught her eye.

Studies of time, space and activity

Yet another area of research has focused on broad parameters that define — and delimit — the reality which participants of a particular cultural group experience. Since Durkheim and Mauss' landmark research indicating how time and space reflect social organization, numerous studies describing the differential conception and use of time, space and activity suggest that there are cultural differences in the structuring of reality.[18]

The Human Relations Area Files testify to wide cross-cultural variability in conceptions of time, whether peoples subscribe to a lunar or solar calendar, varying conceptions of night and day, eclipses and seasons, as well as to the ordering of time (i.e., whether there is a notion of a minimal unit of time [a moment]) or how and if days, weeks, months and seasons might be divided.

Whorf (1940/56) was among the first to suggest that language, thought and reality might vary cross-culturally. He was intrigued by the fact that missionaries and other inhabitants of the area around the Pueblo reported an inability to learn the Pueblo language. After living among the Pueblo for three years, Whorf offered a startling explanation. Pueblo was difficult for English speakers to learn because the realities which they experienced were not commensurate. The Pueblo had a different way of conceptualizing time and space. They lived in present time — and, in language, could only speak in the present. Past and future had no meaning. Furthermore, though the English language contained thousands of words that defined specific spaces (attic, cathedral, kitchen, cave, etc.), the Pueblo language contained none. The Pueblo believed that space existed as a totality and could not be cut up or partitioned in any way. Language could direct one to a place, but the speaker of Pueblo would not think of it as a place separate and distinct from other places.[19]

In later research in which she analyzed the notes and manuscripts of Malinowski, Lee (1950/80) outlined different codifications of reality in terms of differences in conceptions of time and space. She discovered dissimilar organizational principles in the difference between Malinowski's characterization of reality and that depicted by the Trobrianders whom he studied. Whereas Malinowski described the island, the people and their practices and rituals in lineal terms, Lee noted not a single lineal referent in the language of the Trobrianders themselves. Postulating that there are both lineal and non-lineal codifications of reality, she suggested that individuals in any society pattern their thinking and behavior in accordance with the codes of their culture and only comprehend information presented in this code. She speculated that alternate codes can thus lead us to aspects of reality which our own code excludes.

To the Trobrianders words represented self-contained concepts, and events and objects likewise represented a series of beings, not becomings. Objects and events existed unto themselves and did not derive their meaning from their relation to other objects and events. Cause and effect were incomprehensible. Similarly, there were no linguistic distinctions for past and present.

English-speaking peoples, she wrote, at least those steeped in the values of their societies, take the line for granted. It underlies the most cherished assumptions regarding logic, progress, and development. People 'draw' conclusions, assuming that projects begin and papers end. They 'trace' relationships between and among facts. Some events cause others to occur and can thus be predicted. The Western concept of time as stretching back into the past and forward into the future assumes the axiomatic nature of the line.

Lee believed that the coherence of Trobriander experience derived instead from the inherent patterning of the repeated act. For the Trobriander linearity existed in acts of intention that were communally viewed a despicable. Value lay in sameness, in identity and unity with past experience, and change, which was both erosive and devisive, was to be avoided. Like Benedict, Lee believed that organizing principles within the group served to orient individuals to define the reality which they experienced.

Looking at contemporary cultures, Hall (1956 and 1976) saw time and space as frames for organizing activity. He distinguished M-time or monochronic time from P-(polychronic) time. Likewise noting the linearity of Western time, Hall has explained how an industrial society demands scheduling. People who subscribe to M-time prefer to do one thing at a time; M-time emphasizes promptness and segmentation.[20] According to Hall, many other societies operate according to P-time. P-time is characterized by the fact that several things are happening concurrently. P-time systems stress involvement of people and completion of transactions rather than strict allegiance to preset schedules.

Between-group differences in the utilizations of time and space within sub-group populations in the United States have also been examined (Cohen, 1969). Children who are reared in nuclear families appear to adopt an analytic cognitive style, whereas children reared in shared function environments adopt a relational style.[21]

The analytic mode presumes a system of linear components, the perception of time as a continuum or the linear projection of social space. Such an orientation enables an individual to think in terms of cause and effect and to consider the possibility of multiple causation.[22] Cohen has contended that, without the assumption of linearity, notions of social mobility, the value of money, individual 'improvement,' getting ahead and the concept of hierarchies have no meaning. Yet, Cohen notes, 'the requirements for formal abstraction and extraction of components to produce linear continuua are not logically possible within the relational rule set' (*Ibid.*, p. 303). Children who adopt the relational rule set tend to perceive time as a series of discrete moments rather than as a continuum, to see themselves in the center of space rather than in a position relative to others who are moving at different rates through social space and to think in terms of specific rather than multiple causality.[23] Cohen's work suggests that qualitative differences in thinking — and in social processes by which children learn to think — are of major consequence, thus making it important to be knowledgeable of the contexts in which children learn to organize information into meaningful wholes.

In research dealing specifically with black child rearing practices Hale cites Asa Hilliard's core characteristics of Afro-American culture, some of which are summarized below;

1   Afro-Americans tend to respond to things in terms of the whole picture instead of its parts.
2   Afro-Americans tend to prefer inferential reasoning to deductive or inductive reasoning.
3   Afro-American people tend to approximate space, numbers, and time rather than stick to accuracy.
4   Afro-American people tend to prefer to focus on people and their activities rather than on things ...
5   Afro-American people in general tend not to be 'word' dependent. They tend to be very proficient in non-verbal communications (Hilliard, 1976, in Hale, 1982, p. 42).

As this list indicates, several observable characteristics appear to be interrelated: relational thinking, linguistic style, people orientation, and a preferential utilization of time and space.

Research indicates that Black Americans not only tend to approximate space and time (Hall's P-time orientation), preferring involvement with people and completion of activity to segmented schedules, they also have been shown to be people-oriented in terms of valued activity (Greenfield and Bruner, 1969; Heath, 1983). Young (1970) describes white child rearing practices as *object-oriented*. Children are typically provided with a great number of toys and manipulable materials and encouraged to discover properties and relationships. Afro-American children, by contrast, tend to grow up within large family networks with a great deal of human interaction, and objects are considered less important. In her study of a southern Georgia community, Young found back child rearing practices to be *people-oriented*. When a baby reached to grasp an object, the baby's hand frequently was taken and held to the adult's face or a game of 'rubbing faces' ensued. As Young (1970) writes, 'The personal is thus often substituted for the impersonal' (p. 280).

Though the present study had an 'evolving logic' that came from working in two settings over time, other researchers have looked in similar fashion at how time, space or activity is constructed in different settings, in order to better understand the cultural values that provide order for different social groups.

Summary

After a presentation of major theoretical perspectives, cross-cultural studies and social class studies of child rearing within complex societies were discussed and differences between and among groups were further developed through discussion of studies of macrocultural differences, studies of cross-cultural personality and cognitive differences among individuals, and micro analyses of cultural differences in verbal and non-verbal behaviors and in the structuring of time, space and activity.

From the above-cited studies two general patterns seem to emerge. A *collective* orientation is apparent when enculturation occurs in a shared function environment where the focus is on social relations, stressing 'kinship,' interdependency, and cooperation, a holistic world view, relational thinking, and the importance of non-verbal communication. An *individualistic* orientation predominates when enculturation occurs in a nucleated family structure, focusing on manipulatory experience and stressing self-achievement, competition, the ability to abstract parts from wholes, abstract thinking and the importance of verbal communication.

How a child comes to think, to know, to communicate, and to act is strongly influenced by child rearing practices which are themselves conditioned by adaptations made to the exigencies imposed by different social and economic environments. Nonetheless, defining how social structural features affect child rearing practices for different racial, ethnic and social class groups within complex Western society and the meaningful adaptations made to differing environments within the society have been topics of only recent interest.

Though these studies cast light on broad differences in child rearing practices and are suggestive of differences that might be expected in terms of subsequent child behavior, in fact, little is known about the moment-to-moment, day-to-day interactions between children and adults in different contexts. What do adults perceive as their situation in life? How are values and attitudes transmitted to children? How do adults structure their immediate environment? And what subsequent behaviors are observable in the children? In brief, what do adults *do* to orient children to adapt to the world in a particular way? It is these issues which the present study addresses.

Notes

1 Kroeber and Parsons (1958) stress the structural aspect when they describe culture as the 'patterns of values, ideas, and other symbolic-meaningful systems' (p. 583). More recently Harkness and Super (1980) write that the 'anthropological perspective is not only the cultural relativism now familiar to most of us. It is more fundamentally an appreciation of culture as a setting for human behavior. Although anthropologists differ among themselves about exactly what constitutes culture, they share a profound assumption that individual human lives are embedded in a social context that has a structure of its own' (p. 2).

2 Durkheim never again chose to use this typology, and social anthropologists have since shown that the distinction more accurately exists in its inverse. The mechanical-repressive thesis that presumes that, for 'primitive' peoples, law rises from the collective conscience is directly contrary to fact. Only a very few crimes were dealt with by an assembly or by a council of elders. The increasing centralization, bureaucratization, collectivism and nationalism characteristic of the organic-functional form suggest that law is, in fact, more repressive when no longer settled within the family or negotiated between families or clans as it had been in the past (Nisbet, 1974).

3 Aron (1967) summarizes Weber's discussion of four types of action:
   1 Zweckrational action, or rational action in relation to a goal
   2 Wertrational action, or rational action in relation to a value
   3 Affective or emotional action
   4 Traditional action

Significantly, Weber defined *rational* action from the perspective of the knowledge of the actor rather than the observer. In other words, Weber assumed that a person would/could make rational decisions based on the information at hand. Goal-directed action enables the individual to get something he wants. Value-directed action enables a person to act in accordance with his or her beliefs. Emotional action is that action taken because of the feeling state of the moment. Traditional action is action that is habitual or that which is accepted by custom. Weber's ideas have been more fully developed by Talcott Parsons who devised an approach to social systems called functional imperativism (see particularly his discussion of 'voluntaristic action' in *The Structure of Social Action*.) Interestingly, however, Parsons himself has been criticized for not placing enough importance on the actor's ability to interpret, evaluate and select courses of action.

4 DeVos and Hippler (1969) have written:

> Present-day approaches to culture are most often concerned with the influence of culture on the structure and function of comparatively viewed societies. The concept of culture is also used as a means of understanding the influence of different social environments on psychological structures (p. 323).

5 However in an article published the same year in which he investigated Hopi, Navajo and Rio Grande children Dennis (1940) named culture as the major determinant of the fact that these groups develop an ability to walk more slowly than white American children (cited in DeVos and Hippler, p. 331).

6 Whiting and Child used US data that pre-dated the post-war era of permissiveness.

7 Minturn and Lambert's work pre-dates the current study and lays the groundwork for it to the extent that they focused, likewise, upon beliefs and practices as adaptations to specific environments. Where they look specifically at mothers, however, the present study examines child training more generally and demonstrates how adults within a culture transmit their values, attitudes and practices to children. Also, where Minturn and Lambert set out to test specific hypotheses, the present study attempts to show how adult beliefs and practices are consonant with their total life experiences. Such experiences thus influence their construction of alternative social environments.

8 See also the work of William Labov. In 'The Reflection of Social Processes in Linguistic Structure' he notes that the 'shape of linguistic behavior changes rapidly as the speaker's social position changes' (Labov, 1968, p. 240). He observes distinct social class differences in speech and sharp differences between blue-collar workers, white-collar workers and professionals.

9 Ironically, working class individuals and groups also learn to participate in their own oppression through resistance to mainstream norms (see, for example, Willis, 1981; Everhart, 1985).

10 Stack (1975) and Hill (1972) both describe the informal adoption of children within the black community. Many children are raised completely or for a time by a grandmother, aunt, older sister, or neighbor. A young girl frequently will not raise her firstborn, who will be cared for by someone in a network of family and friends until she is considered old enough to be responsible.

11 Piaget himself was not concerned to show 'lags' but rather process.

12 When considering culture and personality or culture and cognition a critical question is the extent to which external forces influence thought. Western researchers have tended to assume that the acquisition of socially valued

behaviors is indicative of 'cognitive competence.' Yet the question of whether development or adaptation is key is strikingly apparent in an example from Langer's survey of developmental theories:

> Evidence for the assertion that the child's level of cognitive development informs (sets the limits to and the potentials for) the range of his imitative conduct is provided by a simple experiment (Kuhn and Langer, 1968). Three-year-old children do not usually perform the behavior they observe when they are told, 'Look what I can do . . . You can do anything you want.' Four-year-olds treated similarly perform aspects of the model's behavior. Both three- and four-year-olds perform the observed behavior when they are told, 'Look what I can do . . . Do exactly what I just did.' The difference, it seems, is that the three-year-olds have not yet developed the cognitive competence to decode the message implicit in the first instruction, that is, to perform the observed behavior. Both three- and four-year-olds understand the second, explicit instruction, and they perform accordingly. By four years, children develop the cognitive competence to understand an implicit instruction to accept behavior as a model (Langer, 1969, p. 175).

The three-year-old children are explicitly told 'You can do anything you want,' yet their failure to decode the implicit request (conveyed through modeling the desired behavior) is viewed by the researcher as not yet having developed 'the cognitive competence to understand . . .' It appears equally likely that the children have not yet been socialized to decode covert requests. By extension, a child enculturated into a group wherein requests are made explicitly would not be likely to display much 'cognitive competence' on such a test.

13 Psychoanalytic theory has exerted the major influence in the formulation of hypotheses regarding personality development. In preschool education, until the 'era of Piaget', Freud was the influence of consequence. Child psychology, the nature of the legal system regarding issues related to children and to child rearing, the nature of child rearing practices, the very language used to describe the experience of child rearing ('toilet training', 'demand feeding', 'Oedipal complex', etc.) all are dominated by Freud's psychoanalytic model.

14 Cognitive developmental theory has grown over the past decades both in emphasis and in importance. This spurt of enthusiasm is indicated by Sears (1975) in his overview of child psychology. He lists the number of chapters dedicated to cognitive process in the five handbooks of child psychology:

1931 — 1 (Piaget)
1933 — 1 (Piaget)
1946 — 0
1954 — 0
1970 — 6

Similarly, Sears and Dowley (1963) note that early childhood education has shown an evolution of objectives in the course of the century. In the 1920s physical health and routine habits were emphasized; in the 1940s socio-emotional growth was stressed, and, since the 1960s cognitive growth and related abilities for success in school have been the primary focus.

15 A complex debate has developed out od this assertion. See, for example, Parsons, 1969, in particular her chapter entitled 'Is the oedipus complex universal?' and Spiro, 1982.

16 Yet another provocative line of enquiry has been the work of critical theorists who have tried to integrate a theory of large-scale social structure to the way in which this structure reproduces itself in the interpersonal experience and personality development of its members (Horkheimer, 1936). Basing her argument on the work of George Lukacs, for example, Buck-Morss (1975) finds abstract formal cognition to be the type of thinking common in Western industrialized societies, societies in which the principles of abstract exchange value (rather than use value) and reification govern production and exchange. The separation of formal mental operations from the perceptual objects which provide the content of thought is seen as the counterpart of the alienation of workers from the object of their production. Progressive alienation is demonstrated by Piaget's protocols themselves which require that children learn to perceive sameness despite changes in appearance. Buck-Morss argues that Piaget's cognitive stages mark progressive assimilation of the structural principles of industrialism; therefore, she suggests, Piaget's contention that these developmental stages are 'universal' would seem questionable. A distinction is made, however, between abstract formalism (Piaget's 'final stage') and abstraction which is characteristic of all human languages (Chomsky, 1968) and all categorical systems (Lévi-Strauss, 1962).

17 Elsewhere Birdwhistell (1967) notes that language is not equally important in all cultures, and, even in a highly verbal culture, most of an individual's time is spent in *non-verbal* interaction with persons and things.

18 For example, Hallowell has written that: 'The cultural patterns of different societies offer different means by which spatial perceptions are developed, refined and ordered. The spatial concepts of different societies also vary with the degree of abstraction attained . . . the variability is correlated with the fact that one set of conditions may demand very little in the way of spatial discrimination of a certain order (for example, measurement), but considerable refinement in other respects (for example, directional orientation)' (Hallowell, 1955/77, p. 147).

19 There has been much debate about the so-called 'Sapir-Whorf hypothesis'.

20 Hall (1976) writes: 'Monochronic time is arbitrary and imposed; that is, *learned*. Because it is so thoroughly learned and so thoroughly integrated into our culture, it is treated as though it were the only natural and 'logical' way or organizing life. Yet it is not inherent in man's own rhythms and creative drives nor is it existential in nature.' As an example, Hall cites the

story of Eskimos working in a fish cannery in Alaska: 'The idea that men would work or not work because of a whistle seemed to them sheer lunacy. For the Eskimo, the tides determined what men did, how long they did it and when they did it. Tide out meant one set of activities; time in, another' (p. 17).

21 Cohen postulates that children develop different cognitive orientations based on the socialization they receive in primary group structures (see the preceding discussion). Middle-class children tend to live in nuclear families, in what she calls 'formal' styles of organization, and to utilize analytic cognitive styles. Lower-class children frequently live in broader family structures and are more likely to utilize relational cognitive styles. In the lower-class community in Pittsburgh where she did her research, Cohen found that functions such as leadership, child care and rights to funds were 'shared' by different family members and not assigned to status-roles. Interestingly, however, Cohen notes that upper-class people likewise tend to utilize a predominantly relational cognitive style.

22 This presumption has a long history. Kant had argued that there were structures (form) that existed independent of content. 'Thus ... the fact that human thought entails seeing objects as occupying time and space is independent of *what* objects are seen; similarly, according to Kant, the notion of 'cause' necessarily means that, if A causes B, then A occurs before B in time (we now know that there are systems of thought for which this is not the case, however: The notions of cause implicit in sympathetic magic, for example, or classical Chinese or Greek thought, and Hegelian dialectics — and not also some notions in modern theoretical biology such as Waddington's notion of the chreod, or evolutionary 'pathway' are causal without specifying temporal relations between cause and effect' (Dolgin et al, 1977, p. 12).

23 Hale (1982) cites evidence that some aspects of Afro-American culture are more accurately described in circular than linear terms.

3 Methodology

In this chapter ethnography is defined and the history of educational ethnography briefly reviewed. Ethnographic method is explained and related to broad issues which the study addresses. Specifics of the study are then detailed and the issues of reliability and validity and the possibilities of generalizability discussed.

Ethnography

Ethnography, as Geertz (1973) explains, is both the process and the product of the study of human culture. Ethnography is what the anthropologist does and also the written record — an ethnography — of his or her labors. It is, in Wolcott's (1975) succinct phrase, 'an anthropologist's picture of the way of life of some interacting human group'. Erickson (1979) uses Bauman's (1972) more elaborate definition. In his words ethnography is 'the process of constructing through direct personal observation of social behavior, a theory of the workings of a particular culture in terms as close as possible to the way members of that culture view the universe and organize their behavior within it' (p. 182).

Qualitative research methodology has operated under various labels: ethnography, participant observation, qualitative observation, case study, or field study. Smith (1977) uses these terms synonomously, while Wolcott (1980) draws a sharp distinction between ethnography, the classic long-term field study with a cultural emphasis, and what he considers to be other forms of qualitative research. Smith notes that ethnographic research (the umbrella term) has been carried out in four general areas: non-Western cultures, contemporary communities, formal organizations and small groups.

Educational ethnography did not become an acknowledged subfield of the discipline until the early 1970s (Diamond, 1971; Ogbu, in press). Roberts (1976) notes that in societies traditionally studied by anthropologists education as such did not take place in formal schools. Diamond gives another interpretation — that the study of schooling, an agent of cultural change in remote colonies, was incongruous with the structural-functional orientation of most anthropologists. The immediate antecedents of educational anthropology lie in the work of culture-and-personality anthropologists who studied how culture affects child rearing practices, and, in turn, how child rearing practices shape culture (Ogbu, in press).

Though writers such as Spindler (1955 and 1963) and Henry (1963) had done early work in the field, the social upheaval of the 1960s was a major spur to the foundation of an educational anthropology. In 1963, funded by the US Office of Education, Diamond instituted the *Culture of the Schools Study Project*. The American Anthropological Association took over the project in 1965 with Frederick Gearing as the Director. Some of the findings and subsequent conference papers were later published as *Anthropological Perspectives on Education* (1971). Edited by Wax, Diamond and Gearing, the volume served as a mobilization effort for later work in the field (Ogbu, in press).

Just as anthropologists have variously described what anthropologists do (Malinowski, 1922; Powdermaker, 1966; Wax, R, 1971; Geertz, 1973; Hymes, 1974) numerous researchers have now attempted to outline ways in which ethnography can address questions crucial to the study of schooling (Wax, M, 1971; Erickson, 1973; Rist, 1977; Smith, 1977 and 1979; Wilson, 1977; Wolcott, 1975; Spindler, 1982; Ogbu, in press). Numerous collections (Wax, Diamond and Gearing, 1971; Roberts and Akinsanya, 1976a and 1976b; Spindler, 1982) and at least two textbooks (Dobbert, 1982; Bogdan and Taylor, 1982) are now available. Helpful overviews include Wolcott's (1975) bibliography and Wilcox's (1982) review.

Ethnographic Method

The ethnographer's task is to apprehend and then to render through description the meaning system of an interacting group (Geertz, 1973). Borrowing from Ryles, Geertz maintains that it is through 'thick description' that the researcher strives to distinguish a twitch from a wink and a wink from a parody of a wink. Unlike 'thin description' which defines a twitch as rapid movement of the eyelid, thick description is concerned with people's attitudes, values and beliefs about what they do. The ideal of fieldwork is thus to live as closely as possible with the host people, sharing their work, thoughts and concerns.[1]

While participating and observing, the researchers will keep extensive fieldnotes, notes which are analyzed while in the field and later when the final report or writing is being formulated. Thus the fieldworker is a person of two worlds — the world of everyday life in which he or she shares and the world of the scholar who attempts to penetrate and understand the patterns of this daily existence. What is ultimately realized is a product of that tension (Wax, R, 1971; Wax and Wax, 1980).

While attempting to depict meaningful patterns of behavior[2], however, the researcher constantly looks for negative cases that might force a restructuring of the model (Glaser and Strauss, 1967) and strives to triangulate data sources by 'checking out' explanations with different people or by looking to see if and/or how observations correlate with interviews and with written documentation in a given setting.

As in anthropology generally, participant observation, interviewing and analysis of documents form the cornerstones of enquiry in educational ethnography.[3] However, researchers have also employed other methods in order to understand school contexts as thoroughly as possible. These include videotaping (Byers and Byers, 1972; Florio and Walsh, 1978; Erickson, Florio and Breme, 1975), film (Spindler and Spindler, 1982), the use of projective measures (Spindler, 1974) and questionnaires (Burnett, 1969; Peshkin, 1978). Recent ethnographies frequently have provided a context which gives such measures an explanatory power they might otherwise lack.

The Method for the Question

A number of descriptive accounts of American education for Black children have been written, both popular (Kohl, 1967; Haskins, 1969; Kozol, 1967; Decker, 1969; Herndon, 1968) and academic (Eddy, 1967; Moore, Jr., 1967; Rist, 1970a, 1970b and 1978; Leacock, 1969; Fuchs, 1969; Smith and Geoffrey, 1968). All of the former are reports by Whites based on a year of teaching in self-contained classrooms in predominantly Black public schools. Each of the latter uses an ethnographic perspective for the study of schools.

Though these studies have set the standards in the field, they nonetheless have limitations. The nature of public schools is such that, in each of the studies, the researcher is more observer than participant. (Smith and Geoffrey, of course, solved this dilemma through their ingenious use of dual 'insider-outsider' perspectives.) Furthermore, the above-cited studies, though pioneering, are based on rather short-term field work experiences; Leacock observed for four months, Eddy for three, Smith for one semester. Even Rist, though his work spanned a full year of kindergarten and a semester of second grade, was typically present only two days per week. Finally, none of these studies attempt to compare directly ways in which educational experiences for Black children might differ from that provided White children. The present study is thus unique in several ways. It is an ethnographic account based on a full year of field work; it is one in which the researcher actively participated with the teachers; it is one of the first ethnographic accounts that compares American preschool classrooms; and, finally, it is one which attempts to compare in-school differences in enculturation in early education settings.

Although researchers have detailed ways in which cultural discontinuity frequently occurs when minority children enter public schools, little is known about the nature of this discontinuity. How is the *patterning* of social life different for different social groups? What social and environmental factors help to maintain and reproduce those patterns? And, since early schooling and social programs for the 'disadvantaged' have received such attention, how must programs such as Head Start function in a given setting: to support 'the culture of reference' (Burnett, 1969) of the school or of the culture of origin?

The question of how cultures are organized has been of interest in anthropology from its beginnings. But, surprisingly, the question of how a culture is transmitted to the progeny of the world's people, so that cultural differences and group cohesion are maintained, is of relatively recent concern. Roberts (1976) notes that it was not until Margaret Mead and other female anthropologists focused on the internal dynamics of families in particular and on childhood education in general that enculturation became a legitimate area for anthropological enquiry. Anthropologists turned to topics related to child development in the 1920s (Mead in Murchison, 1931), but it was probably not until the publication of Mead and Wolfenstein's classic *Childhood in Contemporary Cultures* (1955) that these issues began to be addressed within complex Western societies.

Enculturation is a two-fold process. It is the means by which the individual becomes a part of the group and also the means by which the group is reproduced and perpetuated. It includes the acquisition of skills, habits, values and attitudes. In complex societies 'enculturation' is frequently blurred with the concept of 'socialization', and it is not uncommon for experts to assume that a minority child needs to be 'bicultural', enculturated to the group of origin and 'socialized' to the dominant society (Valentine, 1971). Studies of the enculturation process typically focus on the environment in which people live, the adaptive response made by adults to this environment and the way in which adults prepare and train children to adapt to their life circumstances.

Preschool classrooms generally have not been understood in anthropological terms. More typically it is assumed that a classroom is a self-contained social system, that the teacher deals with content (knowledge), and that the quality of an educational setting is determined by how much he or she 'knows'. Within the classroom, children, as individuals, manifest varying degrees of ability. Yet very recent research has suggested that social organization may be more influential than individual ability in the development of language, cognition and social competence (Mehan, 1978; Ogbu, in press).

There is a need to understand how children develop in different social contexts (Bronfenbrenner, 1976; Harkness, 1980; Harkness and Super, 1980; deLone, 1979), yet little or no work to date has looked at early childhood classrooms as settings wherein children continue to be enculturated into the traditions of an ongoing social group. Ethnography thus may offer a new perspective that could serve to inform the understanding of early education settings.

The Pilot Study

Prior to the current study was a semester-long pilot study, designed as a preliminary exploration of a preschool setting. The emphasis of the research was on developing methods of 'stopping the action' in an environment where the wash of movement, activity and interaction could be overwhelming to the prospective observer.

The Site

The site for the pilot study was a traditional integrated preschool located in an inner suburb of a major midwestern city. The classroom had twenty-two children and two teachers, a male and a female. The depiction of the classroom, teachers and individual children was the result of close and intensive observation, extensive fieldnotes, frequent questioning and in-depth formal interviews. Some document analysis (of the teachers' goals, the school philosophy, etc.) was also incorporated into the overall analysis.

Data Collection

Data were collected over a four-month period (approximately twice weekly, though this was interspersed with week-long periods of more intensive study). Approximately 100 hours were spent 'in the field'. Though much of the time was spent in writing verbatim transcripts of teacher-child, child-child interaction or of the teachers' speech during group time or during a special activity (making playdough, scaling a fish, etc.), work was also done with small groups of children at centers and at group time, and the room was 'charted' in various respects.

These charts included flow charts (see Carini, 1975) of the activity patterns of individual children, diagrams of the activities and materials in the room so that it was possible to see how activities changed over time, and microanalyses of children's language. One aspect of the study was an attempt to discern sex differences in a preschool setting. Another researcher observed the teachers in the room as a preliminary to his dissertation study of men in early childhood education. I observed the children. My results corresponded to the findings of Maccoby and Jacklin (1974) who indicated that, at age three, children entered preschool with clear-cut activity preferences. Boys tended to play in the block area, at the carpentry bench and with wheeled toys; girls tended to select quiet activities (art materials, playdough, puzzles, etc.). Girls also tended to stay with activities longer, while boys would try more varied activities and move frequently from one area to another. Flow charts clearly indicated this differential use of space.

The other researcher noted that the female teacher also spent large amounts of time seated in the art area, while the male teacher tended to move frequently about the room. Differences in disciplining were also noted.

Outcomes and Description

The pilot study resulted in a 150-page monograph which provided the opportunity to explore multiple methods of 'stopping the action' in a preschool classroom. Results of this study have been presented at the Crucial Early Years Conference sponsored by the University of Missouri-Saint Louis and at the Mid-Western Educational Research Association (MWERA) Convention in Toledo, both in October 1980, and, in revised form, at the Second Annual Ethnography in Education Research Forum at the University of Pennsylvania in March 1981.

The Present Study

The Sites

The present study is a comparative study of two early education settings, one a middle-class traditional preschool, the other a Head Start center. The classrooms are both located in an integrated suburb of an American community (named for the purposes of this study, Forest Hills) and are less than one mile apart. (See chapter 4 for further discussion of the settings.)

Role

When I began the study I proposed to do a comparative case study of two classrooms. Visiting the two classrooms selected on alternative days, I took fieldnotes throughout most of the time in which the classes were in session. Though I was ostensibly a 'participant observer' in the settings, the intensive nature of the notetaking precluded much active participation. I would sit with the children writing down nearly every word that I could catch, responding to them when they asked me a question, then immediately recording the interaction. Writing frequently caused me to lose eye contact with the children and thus had a tendency to terminate my interaction with them.

More often I would record child-child and teacher-child interactions. During this time I also did formal analyses of the schedules, of the layout of the rooms and of the children's use of space. Particularly on days when I plotted the activity of children on 'flow charts' (see the discussion that follows), I was not able to take notes on more general activities in the respective rooms.

In both settings I put pen and pad aside each day to assist at snack time, take the children to the restrooms, set the tables, accompany the teachers and children outside, etc. However, conversations with the teacher, though cordial, took place informally and on-the-fly. There was simply no time for extended conversation when class was in session.

At the center I was particularly aware of a certain distance between the teachers and myself. This was magnified late in September when the head teacher resigned to take another position and a new teacher took her place. This teacher was obviously uncomfortable about being 'observed'. I later learned that no one had told her that I would be there, that she felt especially vulnerable anyway, since, she believed, the children were 'out of control' when she came. My notetaking only reinforced her sense of being 'spied upon' in a situation that she was responsible for but did not create.

Concurrently, however, the teachers themselves apparently had decided that I just didn't know what was appropriate to the situation. We would share stories when the children went outside or lay down to rest, but during other times I would begin writing again, if for no other reason to feel purposeful and busy. Since my initial offers of help had been deflected, I felt I had little recourse. One day Ms Washington gathered the children about her for music, telling me first that the record player didn't work, 'But maybe it will this time.' She set the needle on the record, but the song was dull and scratchy. She lifted the needle and looked at me; I wrote something on my pad. Then she set the needle down again. Another ripping scratch as the needle skidded across the grooves. She looked at me again, then put her hands in her lap. 'I guess we can't have music today.' Silence. 'I *could* lead the group in singing, but my throat's sore.' Silence. Only then did I offer to teach the children a few songs. Ms Washington broke into a broad smile. 'Oh, *could* you?' she said, seemingly relieved both that the problem was solved and that I wasn't quite as dense as I seemed.

My feeling of unease persisted. I presented a paper at the MWERA Convention in Toledo sometime during the middle of October. From there I drove to the University of Pennsylvania to confer with David Smith at the Center for Urban Ethnography. After a lengthy discussion of what I was doing, he made several comments which forced me to rethink the project. I had been disturbed that what I was seeing during the initial weeks of observation seemed to reinforce stereotypes. For example, while block shelves and house shelves at the preschool were neatly organized according to size, shape or function, at the center things were frequently simply tossed randomly onto shelves at clean-up time. Dr Smith reminded me that a social setting *always* has an order and that perhaps I still needed to find the order that informed the center. He reminded me that I needed constantly to strive to be aware of my own cultural values and beliefs, that in a very real sense there are different kinds of knowing. His example was graphic: 'Remember that it might be the White kid who knows his address and phone number, and the Black kid who can actually find his way home.'

I was beginning to understand that I had been searching for answers to my questions in terms that made sense to me. But I knew the most important thing that I was to learn all year — that I didn't know anything, and that I needed to begin again. I began visiting the preschool less frequently, spending more and more time at the center.

By mid-November I was going to the center every morning class was in session. I also stopped taking notes in the classroom for that seemed an awkward way to relate to people. I was honest with the teachers telling them that I wasn't sure what I was doing and, if they would have me, I would just work with them for a while. I offered to write my notes later and to try to be of some use.

For several weeks I was 'tested' or at least I felt so at the time. I made materials the head teacher requested, cleaned up after meals, filled the refrigerator, answered the telephone, served lunch. Gradually, we began talking more during naptime, I began staying for lunch and that provided another opportunity for conversation.

The change was gradual, imperceptible, but weeks later I realized that I was a teacher, planning, teaching, cleaning up, sharing chores, concerns, advice and humor. I now typed fieldnotes as soon as I returned home, as many as ten pages on some days, though usually somewhat shorter. The teachers knew that I was writing up events. Later in the year I brought the notes in for them to read as a validity check (see the discussion that follows).

During these weeks, the gradual change in role which I experienced was vital to 'the finding of questions' and to the 'doing of ethnography'. The teachers had had many reasons to mistrust me: I was white, they were black; I was an 'observer', they the observed. Both role differentials have had a history of abuse. What was ultimately of relevance, however, was that we were all women, all working single parents, all struggling daily with the ups and downs of working with small children. Labowitz and Hagedorn make the point succinctly: 'Human observers', they write, 'are either judges or participants'.

Data Collection

In all, I was in the preschool on alternating days for two-and-a-half months. Subsequent to the period of observation, I did intensive interviews with one teacher on several occasions. I worked at the Head Start center from September through May. After the middle of November I was there each day Monday through Thursday when classes were held. The teachers did home visits and attended meetings on Fridays. Approximately 480 typed pages comprise my fieldnotes and related papers from this time, exclusive of the schedules, maps and flow charts that were done early in the year.

Outcomes and Description

The study that follows is an ethnographic comparison of two preschool settings, one a suburban preschool, the other a suburban Head Start center. The analysis is sub-divided into four main areas: the use of time, the use of space, the use of activities and materials, and patterns of teacher-child interaction. The final chapter interrelates the findings of the previous sections.

The study is empirical, based on first-hand observation over a prolonged period of time. Because the formal devices used to illustrate the nature of the enculturation process are embedded in a framework of meaning, the overall paper is ethnographic in nature.

Preliminary results have been presented at the Third Annual Ethnography in Education Research Forum at the University of Pennsylvania in March 1982 and at the annual meeting of the American Educational Research Association (AERA) Convention in Montreal in April 1983. This paper appeared in revised form in the October, 1984 issue of *Sociology of Education*.

Reliability and Validity

Resolving problems of reliability and validity are considered to be fundamental to any research design (Campbell and Stanley, 1963; Cook and Campbell, 1979), yet LeCompte and Goetz (1982) explain that experimental and ethnographic studies approach these issues differently, that some requirements are not necessarily appropriate for both types of studies and that others need to be defined in special ways.

Reliability

Reliability addresses the issue of replicability. External reliability is concerned with whether or not the same constructs would be generated by different researchers in similar settings. Internal reliability asks whether researchers would match the constructs generated from a study in the same way as the original researcher.

As LeCompte and Goetz point out, ethnographic studies are conducted in natural settings and thus even the most exacting attempts cannot replicate a study precisely as it occurred. Much is determined by unique circumstance and by the personalities involved in a given time and place. For these reasons, reliability may only be approached, if not attained, by ethnographers (Pelto and Pelto, 1978; Rist, 1977). However, to the extent that people make culturally mediated adaptations to their life circumstances, to that extent relatively similar patterns of child training should be apparent in other settings. It is therefore imperative that the ethnographer clarify the issues which the study addresses, the segment of the population studied, the time period in which the study occurred, and the methods used.

Issues and segment of population studied

The present study is concerned specifically with the ways in which culture is transmitted in two preschool settings, the ways in which teachers re-create and maintain a given social order and the ways in which they transmit their order to the children in their care. The study focuses on in-classroom phenomena and addresses only peripherally the broader context in which classroom interaction occurs. The study was intended neither to address the inner workings of the bureaucracy that administers the metropolitan Head Start Centers nor to place the preschool within the church community where it is housed.

Time period

The study is based on: (i) a four-month pilot study in a preschool in the same community as the settings discussed here; (ii) two-and-one-half months of participant observation and interviewing in the Harmony preschool; and (iii) concurrent and extended participant observation at the Irving Head Start center for the period of one school year (1980–81). At the beginning of the year, when I was in both settings, I was primarily an observer. Though I would occasionally 'help out', most of my time was spent documenting the settings, the children's activity, actions and conversations, and asking teachers questions on the fly.

The decision to remain for a longer period in the center was based on two cherished assumptions in ethnography: (i) that the researcher goes in to find the question (it took longer to find); and (ii) that one stays in a setting until one understands it. In addition, I felt a sense of responsibility to the teachers. They were helpful to me in my project, and I felt obligated to finish out the year helping out in the classroom. Previous experience with middle-class preschools made Harmony comprehensible in a way that the Irving Center was not, though, in fact, the comparative method made 'taken-for-granted' assumptions apparent in a way they had not been before.

In addition, it took much longer to gain rapport with the center teachers than with the preschool teachers, who had accepted me from the first as a colleague. It was only when I became a complete participant, a co-teacher rather than a 'social scientist' in the center, that the teachers and I were able to speak freely about what we were doing and why. The Head Start teachers had been visibly uncomfortable with my feverish notetaking. When I stopped taking notes altogether, save for an occasional scribble on a piece of paper, they were much more at ease, and the time saved freed me to contribute to classroom proceedings. As the head teacher confided to me with a grin months later: 'When you first came, you sure weren't much use to anybody.'

Methods used

The delineation of time, space and materials as lenses by which to study social organization has precedence in the anthropological literature. However, to my knowledge, such perspectives have never been integrated in this way nor have they been applied to preschool education. When I began the present study I did schedules of each setting to see how time was used each day and how assiduously the teachers maintained designated time frames. I also charted the children's use of space, just as I had previously done in the semester-long pilot study. At that time, however, the charts served to indicate how male and female children used space differentially.

Only by analyzing time and space charts concurrently did I begin to see *patterned* differences between the two settings. The use of activities and materials further supported the growing realization that patterns in each setting reflected different means of reaching different ends. During the course of the school year I was able not only to observe patterns, but, through explanation and example, I was taught the meaning of those patterns. These likewise were recorded in the fieldnotes, so that repeated analysis of the body of fieldnotes collected over the year revealed patterns in the settings that were both repetitive and reticulated. Unlike anthropologists who have found the culture of the school to be inconsonant with the cultures of minority children (Wax, Wax and Dumont, 1964; Spindler, 1982). I was discovering that such constructs could be potent in the study of preschooling, where teachers frequently come from backgrounds similar to the children in their care (Zimmer, 1979) and where values and attitudes are not disguised in the blur of ABCs and the new math.

Williamson, Karp and Dalphin (1977) have clarified what can be expected to result from different research enterprises. Empirical generalizations, they write, can be achieved when the researcher estimates the characteristics of a known population by studying a sample from that population. Analytic generalizations result when a reseacher produces a comprehensive analysis that might be applicable in a variety of social contexts. This is the case, for example, with Whyte's (1943/55) famous study which illustrates the social organization of a street corner gang, demonstrating in turn how the gang is associated with racketeering and political factions in the community.

In April 1982 I wrote a proposal through CEMREL Inc. in response to an REP issued by the Department of Education. The proposed study was an effort to replicate this study by testing the analytic generalizability of the constructs reported here. In order to clarify the race/class distinction, settings were suggested that reflected different socio-economic conditions:

1 A Black inner-city Head Start center
2 A Black suburban preschool
3 A White inner-city Head Start center
4 A White suburban pre-school

A researcher is bound to define procedures and constructs as clearly and as thoroughly as possible. The issue of reliability is not resolved, however, until other researchers and practitioners find these same constructs useful across settings.

Validity

Where ethnographic research tends to be weak regarding issues of reliability, validity is its great strength. Validity addresses the issue of accuracy: to what extent do the constructs generated reflect or represent empirical reality? Internal validity is concerned with the extent to which the constructs generated in the research process relate to what is being observed or measured. External validity deals with the applicability of these constructs across groups.

LeCompte and Goetz note appropriately that 'the claim of ethnography to high internal validity derives from the data collection and analysis techniques used by ethnographers' (*op. cit.*, p. 43). Not only do ethnographers typically spend a long time in the field, collecting data and deriving constructs that match the reality of daily living, they also engage in continual dialogue with people in the setting and thus derive constructs that serve to organize the meanings of participants themselves.

The current study is based on a year of fieldwork, supplemented by interviewing. In addition to the data collection techniques typically used by ethnographers, several additional 'validity checks' have been incorporated into the study.

The teachers knew that I was writing up fieldnotes after I left the center. By March I was bringing the typed notes in for a time as a validity check. I would leave approximately one-third of the sheet blank and encourage the teachers to write comments or to disagree with me. 'There's so much going on sometimes, I can't be everywhere or see everything. Tell me, please, if I missed something or if you think it happened differently than this.' The teachers read these tolerantly but never made any written comments. I later wondered if this was not a manifestation of the same 'togetherness' I was to write about. To differ — or argue — was simply not a part of the relationship(s) maintained by the women in the center. The head teacher would tell me that the notes were 'just fine', though she politely wondered at the fact that I was spending so much time and effort on such a mundane activity. Twice the fieldnotes got misplaced for a time in the reams of paperwork for which the teachers were accountable. I began to wonder if my notes were nothing more than additional paperwork, and, when I no longer brought them each day, they were neither asked about, nor apparently missed.

By the end of the year we had several conversations about what I was seeing. The head teacher especially was encouraging, and, though my constructs were at best ill-defined at the time, she assured me that 'you know what you're talking about'. I asked if she would read the final draft and she agreed.

I also maintained contact with the preschool teachers after leaving the setting and interviewed one in depth on several occasions. She, too, agreed to read the final draft and to proffer her opinion as to its veracity and accuracy. Again the issue of external validity will perhaps someday be addressed in the proposed study cited above.

Notes

1 According to Geertz, analysis involves 'sorting out the structures of significa-
tion' (Geertz, 1973). Elsewhere he describes this 'hermeneutic circle' as
'tacking between the most local of local detail and the most global of global
structure in such a way as to bring both into view simultaneously ...
Hopping back and forth between the whole conceived through the parts
which actualize it and the parts conceived through the whole which motivate
them, we seek to turn them, by a sort of intellectual perpetual motion, into
explications of one another' (Geertz, 1974/77, p. 491). In this way, Geertz

explains, ethnographic interpretation is akin to literary, historical, or psychoanalytic interpretation — or, for that matter, common sense.

2 Mead (1947) notes that social and experimental psychologists deal with a large sample of individuals and tend to work with units of attitudes and behavior, whereas clinical psychologists and cultural anthropologists tend, conversely, to work with a large number of observations on a small number of individuals and thus strive for validity, not from the number of individuals sampled, but through the number and kinds of behavior sampled *that* form a pattern.

4   The Setting

The Community

Forest Hills[1] is an inner suburb of a major American city. Once one of the wealthiest areas of the metropolitan area, it has undergone massive population shifts in the last twenty years. The major precipitating factor for these changes has been the influx of inner city Blacks in the latter-half of the 1960s, a movement both encouraged by city policy and discouraged by municipal restrictions.

The 1960 census lists 203 'non-Whites' as Forest Hills residents. By 1970 these numbers had increased to 9292 Blacks, 257 Chinese, sixty-one Japanese, thirty-four Filipino, twenty-two Indian, 140 'other' and 36,514 White for a total of 46,320. In that year 16.9 per cent of the population was 65 or older. Thus, many white homeowners no longer had children in the schools. By 1980 the overall population had decreased by nearly 4000 individuals for a total population of 42,738. Of this number, there were 23,498 Whites, 18,367 Blacks, thirty-seven American Indians, 582 Asians and Filipino, 352 Spanish and 254 'other'.

The present research began as a comparative study of two pre-school programs in Forest Hills, one a middle-class preschool, the other a Head Start center for children of low-income families. The two schools are less than one mile apart. Initially, the most obvious difference between them was the racial composition of each classroom. The preschool has twenty-three children, aged two years nine months to five and three teachers; the center has twenty-one children in the morning, another twenty in the afternoon, with two teachers. A few children turned four in the first two months of school; for most of the year all but one were between four and five years of age. Teachers and students at the preschool are White, at the center teachers and students are Black.

Though Forest Hills is officially integrated, the differences in racial composition in the two schools is indicative of the de facto segregation reflected in larger community residential patterns. A wealthy, predominantly White, corridor runs east to west along the city's southern flank; the predominantly Black, predominantly working-class section of the city runs east to west along the northern border. A 'gray' corridor, integrated and stable, is believed to characterize the city's center.

The preschool is located in the central corridor but borders the wealthiest section of the city, drawing a number of pupils from this area. Most of the children come from middle- to upper-middle-class professional families. Families pay to send their children to the school. By contrast, the center is located in the northern section of the city, and the children come mainly from working-class, often single parent, families. The Head Start program is federally-funded, and children attend free of charge.

The Harmony Preschool

There is something about a church. Something that inspires awe; something that temporarily transforms the spirit. One leaves the wide, tree-lined boulevard with its massive homes and apartment buildings and the hum of traffic is instantly hushed. Here one treads lightly across the flagstone entrance, catching a glimpse of polished wood and stained glass through padded doors. Yet down the hall children romp and play. Inside a large door another large space opens and invites. The Harmony Preschool is located in an Episcopal Church, a stone, neo-Gothic structure adorned with stained-glass windows and long cathedral chandeliers.

A large room (approximately 70' × 35') is made available for the preschool. The room, though smaller, emulates the structure of the church nave. The same beamed A-frame construction and chandeliers give a feeling of grandeur and spaciousness. Three large windows (with clear panes) and two smaller ones provide more than ample light for the room.

The room is equipped with the staples of the traditional nursery school: sand, water, clay, paint, crayons, scissors, books, blocks, puzzles, 'house' area. Because of the large space, a climbing dome, small trampoline and wooden jungle gym can also be accommodated within the room. During the previous summer, wall-to-wall carpeting was installed in the room (by people in the church), and the teachers must now take great pains to see that paint or playdough does not damage it. A hinged plywood platform has been made and laid on top of the rug. The sand table and easel rest on this platform. The first time I spoke with the Directress she registered her concern: 'Of course, if we can't have sand and water and paint we might as well shut down. Such a restriction would wipe out the program.'

The school accommodates twenty-four children at 'three levels.' The Directress describes the environment as 'an open classroom with a linear family grouping'. Most of the time all of the activities are available to all of the children. Only occasionally, for small group work, trips to the park and snack time, do children break into three groups according to age. At the beginning of the year the children ranged in age from two years nine months to four years six months. The Directress was 'reluctant' about having children under three years of age: 'We're just trying this for the first time. We had a group of very young girls whose parents were anxious for them to start.'

The preschool services a distinctly middle- to upper-middle-class clientele. Though the elementary school in the area is 70 per cent Black, there are no Black children in the preschool. There is one child from India and another whose mother is from Germany. Most of the children come from professional families. Fathers are doctors, engineers, lawyers, university professors. Fifteen of twenty-four mothers work or attend school full-time. They, also, tend to have professional occupations. Parents, typically mothers or the mothers of other children, bring the children to school and pick them up. Three children are escorted by Black women who care for them while their parents work. During the first week children were 'phased in' to school, coming in small groups for forty-five-minute periods with their mothers. I was asked to wait until the second week to begin observation. 'All you'll get is "Look at me, mommy!" Come next week for a proper beginning.'

The school is in session from 9.00 a.m. until 11.45 a.m. each day. Two days per week an 'extended afternoon session' is offered. Four children stay (four others come only for the afternoon), eat lunches they bring from home, rest, and have quiet afternoon activities until they are picked up at 3.00 p.m.

Early in the year the Directress explained that the children generally have 'free play' during the first hour of the morning and 'more structured,' teacher-directed activities during the second. During the time in which I observed at the preschool (and in subsequent visits), however, the teacher-directed activities appeared to only comprise thirty–forty minutes of time: a brief 'morning meeting', clean up, storytime, snack and music.

By the second week of school when the observations on which this study is based were begun, the class was already a functioning social group. Children moved easily between, and among, the various areas in the classroom. The teachers were available at all times, and they talked easily and quietly with the children. A soft hum, punctuated by an infrequent, children shout, characterized the room, the murmur of quiet, purposeful activity.

It seemed characteristic, not surprising, that this preschool should be located within — and a part of — a church, for, in America, these children were, by almost all indices, among the blessed.

The Irving Head Start Center

The Irving Head Start Center, one of seventeen Head Start programs in the metropolitan area in 1980–81, is located in a rented basement classroom in the public Irving Elementary School. The school is a three-storey brick building, constructed in 1930. It accommodates approximately 400 students. The front of the building has a circular drive winding up from a major city thoroughfare.

Typically one enters the building from the south parking lot. To get to the Center one descends a short flight of steps, walks through the cafeteria to the rising smell of steaming pots and a cheerful greeting from the staff. The Center is located in the north-east corner of the building.

The classroom encompasses a large area, approximately 70' × 30'. The walls are masonry block, painted institutional green. The old green linoleum, steaked and worn, has been recently waxed. Large windows line the north wall, but, since no direct sunlight enters the classroom, the low-hanging fluroescent fixtures are nearly always lighted. Pipes are painted but visible above them.

After frequent and unsuccessful attempts to reach the teachers by telephone or at the school, I was surprised one morning early in September to find that the door flung open when I pulled at it. I stood in the doorway, awkward and embarrassed before seven or eight mothers and a roomful of children. Everyone seemed busy, so I sat down on the couch in the entry area.

The table there contained a multitude of pamphlets on social services: health clinics, VD, lead poisoning. Two women, it seemed, were helping mothers to fill out forms. Children, some infants, some older, were playing with toys in the room. Several older children were looking after the younger ones. One child, no older than four, was tending a baby who could not yet walk. Twice she carried him by grasping him around his middle, all flaying arms and legs, and walking straddle fashion to another part of the room.

After several minutes the social worker came over to me and asked if I had a child to enroll in the program. I told her who I was and what I wanted: permission to observe the program and the children. I then asked if I could set up a time to speak with her about what I wanted to do. She asked three questions: With what university was I affiliated? Was I a faculty member or a student? And did I live in the community? Apparently satisfied, she went into an area behind a bulletin board partition where there were desks and a telephone. She called the central office and spoke with someone there for several minutes. Finally, she returned. 'They don't have any problem with what you want to do. Apparently people from your school have done this before. When do you want to start?' I answered, 'As soon as possible.' But she immediately discouraged me. Next week they would just be getting organized ... didn't know yet how many children they had ... boxes to unpack. I told her that I didn't want to be in the way, also that I would like to help out if I could. 'That's great!' she said. 'We get federal funding based on our volunteers.' I was introduced to the head teacher as 'What was your name again? ... would like to volunteer.' We spoke for several minutes. Again I offered to help the next week, unpacking or whatever. She thanked me warmly, 'We don't usually get help like that,' but the next week she never called.

When I arrived the following week, the teacher greeted me at the door. She explained that there was still much to do (she pointed to the teachers' area), unpacking and things, so the children were having free play. The assistant teacher was on the telepone. Most of the children had congregated toward the back of the room, where the house area, rocking boat and large wheeled trucks were located. No paint, sand, water, clay, paper, crayons, or scissors were available, though a few children worked puzzles at one of the small tables.

The teacher walked with me to the far side of the room. 'Boys and girls,' she announced, 'listen, if I have to tell you not to play so roughly, not to hurt each other, we won't have free play time anymore. We'll all go and sit on the red rug and put our heads on our lap.' She then walked slowly back toward the teacher area, stopping three times to speak with individual children.

Four or five boys were running behind large, wooden wheeled trucks, weaving in and out and around children and objects. They could and did move quickly on the slick linoleum surface. The puzzles, the house area, the rocking boat, punching bag and trucks were all in use.

After clean-up there was an extended group time. They did a finger play, sang several songs, talked about fall. Then the children lined up, went to the restrooms, and went outside. When they returned, they washed their hands, walked to the cafeteria for lunch and prepard to go home.

Twenty-one children began the morning program in September; another twenty were enrolled in the afternoon. Ranging in age from one late three to nearly five, most of the children are four years of age. The children are predominantly from low-income families that must indicate 'need' in order to qualify for the program. Most are picked up at home by a human services van and brought to school about 8.30 a.m.; the van also returns them to their homes, leaving the school about 11.30. Afternoon children arrive at 12.30 and leave about 3.30.

The following parameters were defined as attempts to isolate the most potent and observable differences between the two programs described above. These differences have been characterized along several dimensions: different uses of time and space, different uses of activities and materials, and differences in the nature of teacher-child interaction.

Note

1 Names of both places and people have been changed.

5   The Use of Time[1]

Different uses of time suggest different conceptualizations of time. Traditionally educational research has assumed that schools are educational rather than social institutions and that teachers and pupils are individual rather than social beings (Wax and Wax, 1971). That meanings are created intersubjectively and that history and culture help to orient individuals in time and space are basic premises of ethnographic enquiries but ones quite new to educational research as such.

The descriptions of the use of time in the two settings observed suggest that time means something quite distinct in each. The analysis that follows further defines these differences. The use of time (group time versus individual time) suggests that time is allocated differentially either to reinforce the child's sense of being a group member or to encourage him/her to individuate. The perception of time, either as a 'container' or as a 'continuum' further underscores the distinction between tradition-bound means of enculturating to a group and 'future-oriented' means when people believe in — and have experienced — 'growth' and 'development' as positive. What is apparent in a profound sense is that enculturators re-create the realities they themselves experience. This is made more apparent in the discussion of 'peer-centered' and 'child-centered' orientations. It is argued that time is perceived differently and used differently in the two settings because it serves different purposes.

The two settings accomplish different ends. The women in the center have a strong sense of kinship and peer loyalty and a belief in treating children equally. The women in the preschool never doubt that individuality is desirable. Alone themselves much of the morning, they constantly make distinctions between and among children, strive to modify the environment in subtle ways in order to encourage 'development.' Yet in a year of field work at the Head Start center, I never once heard the word 'development' used.

How and why children are enculturated to or away from the group and the ways in which early education environments perpetuate rather than alter these tendencies will be central themes as this study evolves.

On a broad scale the two programs allocate different amounts of time to education because they have different purposes. The Harmony Preschool is, in purpose and design, a preschool, an educational program for the very young that operates five mornings per week. The head teacher describes it as 'an open classroom with a linear family grouping'. Embedded in the phrase are certain oft-repeated assumptions: that an open classroom where children can 'play' is the most appropriate educational environment for young children, that children 'develop' and therefore that different activities are appropriate at different ages, and, finally, that preschool is, or should be, like a family and provide the same nurturance and support (i.e., mothering) that children are likely to experience at home. It appeared in Hess and Bear's (1963) terminology that this program was intended to be 'an extension of the home,' while, to some extent, the Head Start program was intended to be 'an extension of the school'.

At the Head Start center the head teacher's very attempt to define the classroom experience as a preparation for school is constrained by Head Start legislation and policy. Defined as a social service, rather than a purely educational program (McDavid *et al*, 1967; Zigler and Valentine, 1979), time is necessarily diverted to care for the 'total child.' The children have both educational and hearing tests at school. The van regularly picks up groups of children for their medical, dental and lead poisoning check-ups and appointments during school hours. The children attend school only four days a week, so that the teachers will have one day to tend to records (the teachers are responsible for keeping track of absences, check-ups, shots, home visits, expert and ancillary personnel, etc.) and to make home visits. In addition, children are off for all public school holidays, for example, when there is no school for parent conferences, and they are also off for holidays such as Veteran's Day and Columbus Day when the public schools are in session. The sum total of these policies, procedures and contingencies means that the Head Start children have considerably less school time than their preschool peers.

Given a set amount of time in the immediate settings, however, other differences are apparent, the most obvious regarding the allocation of scheduled time.

FIGURE A. Comparison of Schedules[2]

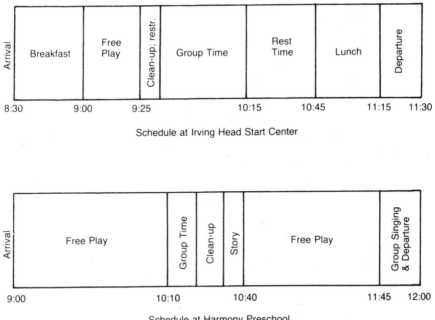

Schedule at Irving Head Start Center

Schedule at Harmony Preschool

Though both programs run for nearly three hours, time frames differ radically and the types of activities within the frames are strikingly dissimilar.

FIGURE B. Time Allocations for Activities

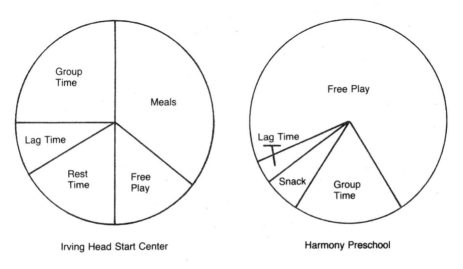

Irving Head Start Center   Harmony Preschool

71

Meals

Because Head Start legislation guarantees children two meals per day, time is necessarily allotted for breakfast and lunch in the morning, and for lunch and snack in the afternoon. These meals frequently take about one third of each group's total time at school.

Breakfast is provided by a catering company and consists mainly of small boxes of dry cereal (Cheerios, Rice Krispies, Corn Flakes, etc.) and milk, and juice in a plastic container. Late in the year, when the teachers complained about the lack of variety, white bread and butter and jelly, sliced American cheese, fruit cocktail or applesauce were occasionally substituted. The children eat breakfast at small tables in the classroom.

Lunch is provided in the elementary school cafeteria. About 10.45 a.m. (though frequently later) a wheeled metal cart would be pushed from the kitchen. It contained individual plastic trays, small cartons of milk, and usually a pan of half sandwiches, two metal bowls of vegetables and a dessert of some kind — apparently the 'hot meal' that Congress has legislated.

The children line up in the classroom, the boys in one line, the girls in another. They are expected to walk quietly into the cafeteria. Places are set (with a paper napkin, a straw and a plastic spoon or fork). The children choose their seats at random; only occasionally, are certain children assigned to seats. Once seated, they are to sit quietly and wait to be served. Teachers dish the food onto trays and serve them.

During the first three months of school the children were responsible for taking their trays to the trash cans and throwing away their milk cartons, napkins and utensils. Late in November, the head teacher decided that, if the teachers took the trays from the tables, there would be less spillage and confusion. For the rest of the school year the teachers removed the trays, and the children waited until the tables were cleared before they again lined up for the return trip to the room.

The preschool children eat breakfast and lunch at home. Typically snack time comes after storytime and before either small group time or the trip to the neighborhood park. 'Snack' is perceived as an opportunity to introduce children to a variety of foods — and to expand their vocabularies. Interestingly, snack time is also a time when children are divided into age groups. Elizabeth sits with the oldest children ('the fours'), Suzanne with the middle-age group, predominatly older threes, and Roxanne has a small group of children three or younger.

The teachers' behavior toward the children differs somewhat, depending on the age of the children. During this time Elizabeth might encourage the children to discuss their summer trips, while Roxanne would be more inclined to speak in lilting, slightly condescending tones and require a minimum of social interaction: 'We're having pineapple juice today. See, it is yellow. Here is some pineapple juice for Anna ... some juice for Matthew, some for Karen ...'[3]

Free Play

Perhaps the most striking difference between programs is the different amount of time spent in 'free play'. The term itself is used in both settings, but, in fact, has different meanings. 'Free play' at the center is a time for children to play alone while the teachers tend to other duties. For much of the year the head teacher would assign children to specific areas for the twenty-five to thirty minute block of time. 'Free time' to her means a time to be free of responsibility for the group and time for the group to be free of adult direction. During this time the teachers generally retreat to teacher space, make phone calls, do paper work, fill the refrigerator or get materials ready for group time or for a group activity.

By contrast, at the Harmony preschool children move about freely and freely choose the activities that interest them. (See the discussion that follows on the use of space.) Though a teacher may ask a child if he or she would like to do something else, I frequently observed children decline. Within these two extended blocks of time children are granted a good deal of autonomy. They generally can make their own decisions, define their own activities, and work at them until they lose interest or reach closure. On occasion, a teacher will attempt to interfere when she feels that the activity the child has chosen is not 'purposeful'. However, it is usual for the decision to persist or desist to be left up to the child.

During the first 'free play' period as many as twelve centers are available. All three teachers are at centers talking with individual children. During the second 'free play' period the group frequently walks to a nearby park where swings, slides, tunnels, etc. are available. The three age groups are again evident, each group, supervised by one teacher, holds onto a long rope to cross the street, then walks down a grassy hill to the playground.

The head teacher at Harmony explains that the teachers' main function is to first orchestrate the environment and then to maximize the use of it for individual children. The free play time is, in effect, the purpose of the morning, a time for children to freely choose from a variety of activities that the teachers value and therefore provide.

Group Time

At Irving each day an extended period of time is set aside for group instruction. When children return from the restrooms after clean-up time they gather on a red rug and wait for the teacher. Children frequently have to wait as many as ten minutes during these transition times while the teacher leaves to answer the telephone or tend to an unexpected visitor.

Typically the teacher begins by taking roll with each child respond-ing 'here' as his/her name is called. For most of the year three lessons predominated: one having each child recite his or her address, phone number and birthdate (see the subsequent section on teacher-child interaction), another having each child recognize his or her printed name on a card held up by the teacher, and finally, after the first of the year, familiarizing the children with the calendar. Children are ex-pected each day to know the month, day and year. After individual children are asked 'What day is it?' 'What month is it?' the group recites in unison several times: 'Today is Wednesday, February 9, 1981.' Generally if one child is asked a question the same question is asked of every child in the class. Later in the year more varied activities were in evidence, though the above lessons were repeated each day for months. Group time frequently concludes with a story, a story record or a record. A child usually holds the book and turns the pages when the record plays. The same stories are listened to over and over. Music, also, is frequently listened to silently. On occasion it is necessary for the teacher to put on a record and leave the area.

During group time children are expected to listen attentively and, when appropriate, to converge on the 'correct' responses to the teacher's questions. The head teacher believes that group time is the time when children learn. Field notes record a frequent remark: 'You are not here to play: you are here to learn something!' The teacher criticizes the supervisor's encouragement of play as 'just babysitting'.[4] She believes that what children really need is to know something: 'If they don't know their name, address and phone number, the kindergar-ten teacher will think they are stupid — and think that I didn't teach them anything!' This concern encompasses the children's general behavior as well, for she likewise sees group time as 'getting the children ready to listen to the teacher'.

At Harmony group time is relatively brief and cut up into three even shorter segments because 'the children have such short attention spans, you know'. The first time when the group convenes typically occurs one hour and ten to fifteen minutes after the children arrive (i.e., after the first extended period of free play). A teacher takes roll silently or tells the children they can 'count heads' with her. She points to individual children and counts slowly, then asks the children who is missing.

The purpose of the first group time changes as the year progresses. Early in the year 'meeting' time is a time to explain to children how the room is to be used and how the clean-up period that is to follow is to be effected. Later, as each week one color is stressed, meeting time is an opportunity to introduce things related to the color theme. For example, during green week Elizabeth introduces a variety of vegetables:

> Does anyone know what this is called? . . . Yes, a cucumber. Is it light green or dark green? This looks like a cucumber, but it has a name all its own — squash. There are so many kinds of squash. What special name does this have? (No response.) This is zucchini. This is? . . . Yes, lettuce. And these? . . . These are green beans. Is this one cooked or not cooked? Green beans are good to eat cooked or not cooked. If it was cooked, it would be *softer*. Can anyone think of another word for not cooked? . . . Yes, *raw* . . .

Often science topics are introduced at this time: a kind of insect, a pineapple plant, etc. Usually the teacher asks the children if it is a cloudy day or a sunny day. A white paper cloud or yellow sun is then affixed to a calendar, though I never observed any lesson which attempted to explain what a calendar was. After about ten minutes the group adjourns for clean-up time.

The children are encouraged to use the restrooms and then convene in the book area for a story. One of the teachers sits in an overstuffed chair and reads a book, holding it up so that the children can see the pictures. Again, this period is quite short.

Occasionally, the children meet again with their age groups after snack to discuss a special topic, for example, an upcoming fire drill. Children are again separated according to age so that the teachers can engage them in what they consider to be 'developmentally appropriate' tasks. The head teacher explains, for example, that the oldest group will study the body later in the year and take a trip to the museum to see a program on the human body. 'Three year olds', she confides, 'are simply too young'.

Finally, just before their parents arrive the children again gather together, each upon a 'sit upon,' this time in a circle. One of the teachers plays the guitar and short nursery songs are sung: 'Twinkle,

twinkle, little star,' 'I'm a little teapot,' etc. Why these songs? 'The children already know them or can learn them easily. Since they are familiar, it is helpful to the child to make the transition from home to school.' And, since these songs are sung as the mothers arrive, they also seem to reassure them that their children are 'in good hands,' and, in fact, doing what they themselves would do.

Rest Time

At the center, though rest time is posted as a ten-minute block of time (on the official schedule), in fact, it lasts an average of about thirty minutes. Lights are turned off, and the children stretch out on rugs, towels or mats on the floor. Observing in four other half-day preschools for middle-class, predominantly White, four and five year olds in the same community I found that no time was allocated for resting.

I was told that children would be required to rest in kindergarten and that it was important that they get used to the expectations that they would encounter in school. As the year progressed, however, I realized that this 'time' served other functions as well. It was a much needed break for the teachers who were responsible for forty children in the course of their eight-hour work day and responsible for their own children and extended families in their 'off' hours (see the discussion that follows.)

The above descriptions serve as a basis for speculation about the teachers' structuring of events.

Group Time/Individual Time

One of the more obvious observations that one can make from the above data is that the Head Start children spend considerably more time 'grouped' than do the preschool children. They eat as a group, wait as a group, sit quietly together for an extended 'group time,' and rest together. They line up and go to the restrooms and to the cafeteria as a group as well. Approximately two hours and fifteen minutes each day is spent doing what others do.

The same amount of time is spent by the preschool children 'doing their own thing.' The time allotted for free time is reflective of the teachers' general orientation toward individualism. 'We try to find out where a child is', the head teacher had explained to me early, 'and take him further'. Her remark belied underlying assumptions that guided many of the actions of the teachers in the classroom. Children were 'in different places'. Therefore, the teachers' job was to create a 'rich environment' that 'met the needs of all the children' and to 'facilitate their individual development'. Free time was a time to individualize instruction, and snack time and the occasional small group time were times for children of the same age and ability to be together, engaging in what were considered to be developmentally appropriate tasks.

Children's Time at Task: Scheduled or Fluid

At the center it appeared that time was like a series of containers. Each time frame existed unto itself; each was defined by its activity. Though the head teacher was required to post a lesson plan each week, the fact was that events within each frame of time seldom changed much.

The supervisor was treated much like a landlord or a social worker might be. Her power was acknowledged, and surface attempts were made to do what she wanted (a schedule was posted, lesson plans made, certain activities ostensibly provided, etc.). However, such plans on paper did little to regulate the daily life of the classroom. On several occasions, an 'open classroom' was created upon her arrival and maintained until she made her departure. The teachers knew what she expected and merely pretended to implement 'her' program in her presence.

More typically each day was much like any other. The children arrived, had cereal and juice for breakfast, sat on the red rug until assigned to an area for free play. The same blocks and toys were out all of the time. (It was not until much later in the year that these began to change slightly.) During 'free play' each day the teacher took care of other responsibilities while the children played. After going to the restroom, the same group time activity recurred day after day: name, address, phone number. (See the discussion that follows.) And each day a 'rest time' of at least thirty minutes occurred before lunch and preparation for the trip home. Each of these time frames, in short, had characteristics of what anthropologists might call ritual events.[5]

The preschool likewise had events scheduled at certain times. However, the two extended blocks of 'free play' time made variety within an established order possible. During the first period, this variety, as conceptualized by the teachers, was not random but rather continuous. Two of the teachers had taught there for several years, and the other had taught there the previous year. Together they had a sense of what should happen in the course of the year and, though plans might be modified somewhat, there was general agreement that there was an overall plan that would unfold as the year progressed.

Early in the year the teachers introduced primary and secondary colors (my terminology). One color was emphasized each week. They believed individually and as a group that children learned through action and that real life activities were a powerful means of orienting children to notice many aspects of their environment. As explained above, children were shown green vegetables during green week. They cooked vegetables, cooked also 'green eggs', and the teacher read the well-known Dr. Seuss book 'Green Eggs and Ham', That week the playdough was green: dark green and white paint was at the easels, as well as light green paper. Children helped to make green yarn necklaces with green triangles affixed one day, green fringe of construction paper on another. The science table contained some limes, a celery stick in water and another in water dyed with red food coloring. Snack each day focused on something green: green eggs, green apples, green jello, limeade, etc. Flavor (lime) was distinguished from color (green). On the last day of the week parents were asked to remind their children to wear something green. Of 23 children only two girls showed up in clothing that did not reflect the theme. The teachers quickly tied green ribbons in their hair. These activities took place in an environment that was familiar, yet subtly changing in ways that the children themselves could discover (see the discussion below). A year-long plan thus introduced children to an environment that became increasingly complex and differentiated.

Yet children were also perceived as 'developing.' As explained above, children were grouped according to age so that 'age appropriate' activities could be provided. In small groups teachers could further individualize instruction.

However, one needs to hone in still more closely to see how the teachers were constantly making judgments about where a child was (in terms of interest and ability) and where he or she might go. Elizabeth, especially, had a knack for individualizing at the puzzle table.

Elizabeth to Joey: 'This is called a "Tumble Tower," Joey. We need to make a marble sit in the hole . . . Now the way you work this is to turn it till one slips in the hole. Come on, Sara, I'll find something just right for you.' [She hands Sara, a young three, a simple puzzle.] *To David*: 'An ear is missing. The poor man won't be able to hear. Find his ear.' Glen comes over to help Chris match colored squares. 'You match it here, O.K.? he says. 'O.K., now you match the orange one.' *Elizabeth*: 'You are

REALLY being helpful to another person.' 'Yeah, we're sharing.' He turns back, 'Now match this one.' [He takes Chris' arm and moves it to the light orange square.] Chris proceeds to match others and Glen slips away. Chris is so absorbed, he appears not to notice. When he finishes, he is very pleased. Elizabeth exchanges the color squares for number squares. 'Hey,' Chris says, 'this is all mixed up!' *Elizabeth* responds: 'It *is* mixed up. Can you find the numbers?' [Earlier Chris had repeatedly counted the colors and the holes.]

Thus, within the group, children were perceived by the teachers as different people, in 'different places', and developing at different rates. However, for each child, development could be facilitated by the teachers through multiple interactions in the course of the ongoing drama of classroom events.

Teachers had several methods of keeping track of the development of individual children. Two bulletin boards hung on opposite sides of the room. A space was designated for each child by a name card that the children themselves were encouraged to recognize. (Teachers helped the children pin up their own work.) Thus, at a moment's glance, teachers could tell who had not painted on a given day nor done any work at the craft table. Twice I observed Elizabeth 'checking' individual children. On one occasion, she was moving about the room with a handful of small colored plastic bears. She would zero in on a child: 'What color is this?' she would ask. 'And this? And what color is this bear?' Then she would return to the puzzle table and make note of which children did not know certain colors and which colors they seemed not to recognize.

Adult's Time at Task: Peer-centered or Child-centered

Although peer groups appear in all societies, their relative importance varies. Over time, as I worked daily in the center, I became aware of a tremendous social support among the teachers. If one teacher left the room to escort a child to the restroom, the other would move quickly but quietly to complete the task that had been interrupted. When before Christmas I started to feel overwhelmed (for example, cleaning up some mess of paper, paint or playdough that I had done much to generate), I would realize that the other teachers had left their chores, apparently sensing my need, and moved into my area to quickly put it in order. I was frequently to comment on this in my notes.[6] This sense of silent cooperation and mutual assistance was, if not alien to my experience, at best an infrequent occurrence.

Early in the year, the teachers had attempted to socialize me. I had sat for weeks watching people and taking profuse notes but I was, as Beverly was later to tell me, 'not much use to anybody'. After a month the social worker decided that it was time to find out why I was there. I confided to her honestly that I wasn't sure what I was seeing. 'You know,' I had said, 'I feel uncomfortable about just taking notes. I think I'm missing a lot by not participating more'. 'Well, you're lucky that you're here. Some places wouldn't let you in the door'. She let me know inadvertently but clearly that I was to use my privilege with discretion. A few moments later she said: 'We all have problems. We all have times when we need others to cover for us'. The aide had overheard and had immediately chimed in: 'Like when you're not here. I tell people you just left. I always tell them that, so they think you're on the job'. And Saundra had countered:

> Well, like when my baby was sick. Who else can take him to the doctor? They know down there [the central office] that we don't make much and might go shopping sometime during work hours. It's O.K. as long as we cover for each other.

Candi (the aide) gave the summative statement: 'My momma taught me long ago that we gotta stick together. No matter what, just stick together'.

It was many weeks before I began to realize the import of these words. Throughout the year I was taught how to 'cover for each other', how to throw up a smoke screen that gave the appearance of conforming to authority while, behind the scenes, the peer group maintained a quite different social order.

But there were other manifestations as well. Candi was frequently ill but always came to school, so as 'not to let you down'. And Beverly came one morning and immediately began to throw up. 'I knew I was sick', she moaned, 'but I thought I could make it through the day'. Personal concerns frequently gave way to group needs.

By the same token, the group focus that I observed in the classroom appeared to have a broader socializing function. Teachers spent time working together, talking together, keeping track of family and friends on the telephone. Children were constantly supervised, but the primary focus of attention appeared to be on other adults who shared the same concerns, responsibilities, and frustrations[7]. In this context, it seemed appropriate that children should be encouraged to perceive themselves as group members first, individuals second. In fact, nothing was quite so unpleasant and frustrating for the teachers as the frequent 'tattling' of the children. During rest time a child might come up to one of us as we talked quietly among ourselves. 'Jason hit me', or 'Charisse keeps putting her foot on my blanket'. 'When will these children grow up!' Beverly would mutter between clinched teeth. One implication was that adults who work together know better.

To draw an absolute distinction between a peer orientation and a child orientation is, obviously, too simple. At the Head Start center teachers were frequently engaged with children, just as at the preschool teachers frequently spoke with each other. The point here, however, is that the major focus of attention appeared to be different in the respective settings.

Whereas the Head Start teachers value and practice reciprocal relations among peers, the preschool teachers assume that their primary function is to establish relationships with the children and to facilitate their growth. Case histories reveal, however, that this is not merely a matter of educational training or a knowledge of psychological principles. Rather it is an orientation that reflects their own socialization; each teacher had been the product of a nuclear family where the mother had not worked and where she had been the principal child-rearer in the home.

The very nature of the activities that the teachers provide means that they will spend a good portion of the morning with children and, conversely, be separate from the other adults, re-creating the isolation of the middle-class American housewife. Ten to twelve distinct areas are evident in the classroom, and the three teachers are 'stationed' at different centers. Though there is some movement into other areas, I most frequently observed the teachers at the playdough table, at the crafts table and at the puzzle table. I was told that at these centers language learning could be maximized. Teachers typically help children 'clean up' in different areas of the room; they sit with different age groups of children at snack, work with the same age groups of children at 'small group time', walk to the park leading three different ropes of children. Only at the park, where children play with only occasional adult assistance, is it possible to carry on a somewhat extended conversation with other adults. In the context of the classroom, the middle-class nuclear family is re-created in miniature.

Notes

1 See Karweit (1981) for a detailed review of the use of time in educational settings.

2 Diagrams of time allocations in the respective settings are based on a random sampling of schedules over time. In fact, the teachers in both settings settled into a routine, so that these allocations did not change greatly from one day to the next. Though an 'official' schedule was posted in the Head Start center, teachers did as they saw fit in the day to day. The preschool teachers did not post a schedule.

3 Bruner (1978) describes how language emerges as a procedural acquisition in context. Caretakers are shown to modulate their talk with children through their intuitive understanding of the children's responsiveness, simplifying when necessary and 'upping the ante' when a child comprehends a simpler form.

4 Joffe (1977) likewise has noted the differing concepts of learning for Black and White parents and staff. In her study of the Early Childhood Education program in Berkeley she explains that Black and White parents had different expectations of the center and used it in different ways. While Black parents wanted their children to have an academic program during their working hours, White parents saw the center as a family program for both children and parents.

5 In fact, this distinction may be more apparent simply because of the age range in the classroom. However, there was one three-year-old in the Head Start center who was not treated differently. And it was apparent that the children had a range of developmental differences: some scribbling, some doing near schematic drawings, some barely able to hold a pencil, while others could already write their names. These differences were generally not taken into account, since the same activities were provided for all the children.

6 Though Beverly was considered the 'head' teacher by the Head Start administration, she did not act as an authority figure within the classroom. She made out the schedule and did what was required of the person 'in charge.' However, with us she was careful to maintain a sense of equality. Rather than tell us to do anything, she would say 'I wonder if . . .' Or 'What would you think if . . .' Or 'How could we . . .?' All in all, what transpired in the classroom was a community effort. This seemed to be the case in the preschool as well.

7 In fieldwork among the Koya of southern India, the Luo of Kenya, the Samoans and the 'Black' Americans of California, Slobin observes that: 'Mothers do not spend much of their time speaking to children and that the major input of the language acquisition device seems to be the speech of older children. It seems that the isolated American middle class home, in which a mother spends long stretches of time alone with her children may be a relatively rare social situation in the world' (Slobin, 1968, in Serpell, 1976, p. 64).

6   The Use of Space

A classroom is a space with certain measurable dimensions. In it, desks and materials are arranged presumably to maximize learning. A classroom has a certain form. Yet Howard Becker has succinctly stated the difference between what we have been conditioned to see and the difficulty of looking beyond it:

> We may have understated a little the difficulty of observing contemporary classrooms ... it is first and foremost a matter of it all being so familiar that it becomes almost impossible to single out events that occur in the classroom as things that have occurred even when they happen right in front of you ... it takes a tremendous effort of will and imagination to stop seeing only the things that are conventionally 'there' to be seen (Becker, cited in Wax and Wax, 1971, p. 10).

By the same token, a preschool classroom will have certain 'givens': small tables and chairs, blocks, puzzles, books, and, frequently, sand, water, paint and a house area. Their uniform nature, however, belie underlying differences in form and function.

The descriptions that follow illustrate that the way in which space is utilized is reflective of the predominant mode of adult-child interaction in each setting. At the Harmony Preschool adults and children share the same space, while at Irving Head Start a separate space is designated for the teachers only. The spaces likewise serve different functions, that is, they are used differently by the children in the respective settings. Two examples from each setting demonstrate that children at the preschool, to a large extent, individualize their own curriculum (within the options available) by moving freely through space, while children from the center spend most of the morning in the same space as other children. It is also shown that, despite the flux, the preschool children are able to maximize their interactions with adults, both gaining access to the teachers' attempts to individualize instruction and gaining attention for their individual efforts.

Form

The Harmony Preschool is a large, open room sectioned into different areas thought to be conducive to the development of physical and cognitive skills.

FIGURE C. Floor Plan of Harmony Preschool

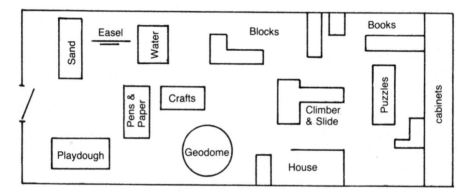

The environment is carefully planned and modified slightly from week to week. For example, a balance beam is set up next to the sand table one week; the beam is pushed against the wall to make way for a water table the next. (See the subsequent discussion of materials and activities for a description of the various areas.) The teachers keep material not in use in large cupboards against the back wall. These are unlocked each day, and different activities are set up in the various areas.

Notably, teachers and children share the same space. No separate area or desk is sectioned off for the teachers only. This utilization of space appears to be a physical manifestation of the form of social interaction practiced in the classroom. Each teacher sits at a small table with a group of children, moving on occasion to another area, frequently at a child's request. A teacher might briefly leave a group of children to remove a painting from the easel or to assist a young child with a paint smock. Groups are not static, however, for the children themselves move in and out of groups at will, sometimes working with this teacher or that or playing alone or with other groups of children.

Though the space itself is approximately the same size, the Irving

Head Start Center has an overall different configuration. The room is divided, not quite in half, into two domains, delineating through the placement of a desk, shelves and bulletin board, a distinct space for the teachers and one for the children.

FIGURE D. Floor Plan of Irving Head Start

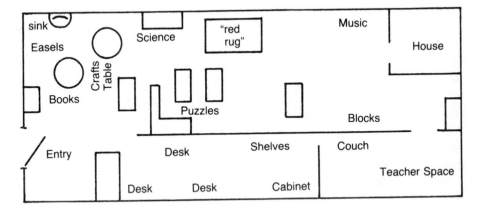

The teachers' area contains the teachers' belongings and materials provided by the central office for the implementation of the program. Here there are three large desks, and a large and small file cabinet. In addition, shelves hold materials, games, eating utensils. A bookcase holds books and records not in use and a large cabinet that can be locked holds supplies of various sorts. Many of these materials are intended to teach specific information regarding body parts, holidays, the calendar, etc. Most have not been purchased by the teachers (who are both new to the center) and are seldom, if ever, used.

A quite separate space is designated for the children. At the beginning of the year field notes make frequent reference to the fact that, though the teachers enter the children's space, children intuitively appear to regard the teachers' area as 'off limits.' The division appears to be a visual manifestation of the type of teacher-student, adult-child interaction that prevails in the classroom. The teacher's role, as defined by Head Start administrators, is not confined to educating children, just as, in many Black homes, women are not only child rearers and trainers, but also the persons primarily responsible for maintenance, exchange of goods and services, management of resources, etc.

In the classroom the teachers are constantly busy, but their efforts are spread out across an array of tasks. Time is spent preparing food, cleaning up, stocking the refrigerator, talking with parents and supervisors on the telephone, writing notes to parents, maintaining records, speaking with health and nutrition officials, speaking with one another, decorating bulletin boards, preparing materials. Many of these duties are carried out in 'teacher space'. When teachers enter 'children space' the specifically educational tasks proscribed tend to take place through teacher directives to the group (group time learning addresses, phone numbers, birthdates, group activities such as coloring projects, etc.).

Function

At Harmony, the teachers believe that they perform a primarily educative function in the classroom. In the 'traditional' nursery school this means creating an environment conducive to learning and facilitating individual development. Although the teachers 'create' the setting (and thereby determine and delimit the choices available) a good deal of autonomy is granted to the children. Figure E illustrates how one child, a four-year-old girl, utilizes the space one day early in the year.

> Sue begins the morning working at the puzzle table with Elizabeth (teacher 1). Here she works an eight-piece puzzle, a shape form board, a five-piece table setting puzzle, and, finally, a 'Big Bird' puzzle with eleven pieces that Elizabeth provides. After about fifteen minutes she spies a baby buggy and leaves the table. (She has completed the puzzle and put it away.) She briefly pushes the buggy, then runs again to Elizabeth: 'I want to paint.' Elizabeth tells her that Roxanne (teacher 2) is by the easel and that she will help her. Roxanne helps Sue put on her smock. Four minutes later, Sue announces to Roxanne, 'I'm finished.' Roxanne then helps her remove her smock and hang her painting on the bulletin board under her name. She then moves to the 'scissors table' and begins cutting small paper with a pair of scissors. Suzanne (teacher 3) is stationed at this table. In a very short time Sue makes contact with her as well. She holds up a square and says to her, 'Look, a triangle!' She has a grin on her face, half teasing, half attention-getting. She has been in the classroom less than one half hour, yet she has already completed approximately seven different activities and interacted with all three teachers.
>   Ten minutes later Sue moves to the playdough table just as Elizabeth begins to talk with a small group of children there. She says something to her, but I don't hear the full statement. In

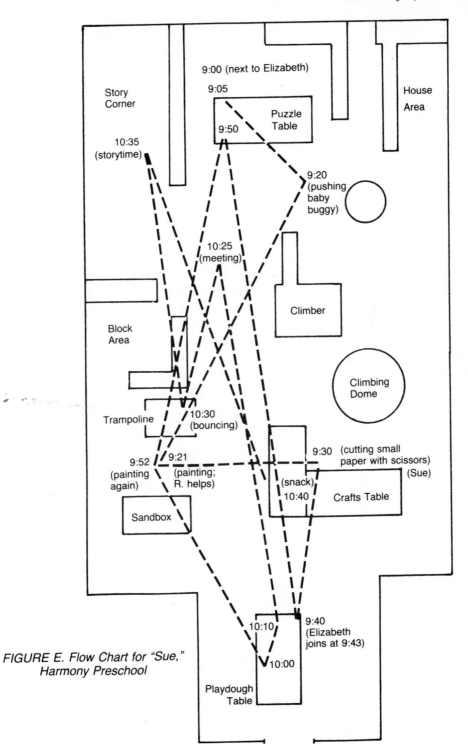

FIGURE E. Flow Chart for "Sue,"
Harmony Preschool

the next few minutes, Sue describes what she makes ('a plum pie', a 'nest') and chats with the group. She frequently vies for the teacher's attention. 'I went to the farm and saw a pink egg', she tells Elizabeth. 'Look at my big snake!' she says, laughing. And shortly after, 'Look at my big ball!' Sue, like numerous other children in the room, seems to have apprehended that the way to get an adult to notice her is to produce frequent, seemingly unique responses.

Sue returns briefly to the puzzle table to work on a graduated shape puzzle. No adult is in the area, however, and this time she does not complete the task. Leaving after two minutes, she returns to the easel. Roxanne again helps her on with her smock. She runs to Elizabeth: 'I don't want my barrett'. After painting, she removes her own smock, and she returns to the playdough table, though to a different seat. Again, she directs her comments to the teacher: 'Ann ate some playdough!' This time she is intent on what she is doing and speaks less, though she does move to a seat closer to Elizabeth. When I get up to leave, she makes eye contact with me: 'Look at my giant ball!'

By 10.25 a.m. a meeting is called briefly; it quickly dissolves into clean-up time. Sue participates half-heartedly and ends up bouncing and giggling with Jennifer on the trampoline. This is virtually the first time she has paid much attention to another child in the room. The children are called to the book area for a 'quiet book time'. Some children go to the restrooms. Soon a teacher reads the group a story. At 10.40 a.m. Sue sits next to Jennifer at snack time. Both children are in Elizabeth's group. During snack, Sue admonishes Ann again: 'You can't talk with your mouth full!' At 10.48 a.m. Elizabeth asks her group if anyone needs to go to the bathroom. 'I do!' Sue concurs and runs off with several other children. At 10.50 there is a music circle, and shortly after, Sue joins Elizabeth and her group, grabs a section of the rope and begins the customary fall stroll to the park.

Sue has learned to work independently. She can select, begin and end activities on her own initiative. Despite the fact that there are twenty-three children and only three teachers, Sue has also learned to maximize her interaction with the adults in the classroom. Much of her behavior and spoken language is directed toward getting adult attention and approval. Her statements tend to express what she wants and what she did: 'I want ...', 'I'm finished ...', 'I don't want ...', 'I made ...' When her actions don't result in teacher comment, she verbally directs adults to notice: 'Look. a triangle!' 'Look at my giant ball!' She knows how to get adult approval and 'tattles' on Ann when she does something that implies disapproval: eating playdough, talking with her mouth full.

Sue, I was told, is 'naturally' gregarious, the middle child of an active outgoing family. She uses the space expansively, in part, perhaps, because she had attended the school the previous year. Such was not the case with Chris, a young three-year-old new to the school, whose actions I followed on the same day.

Chris is a large child with reddish blond hair and sallow eyes. He has some difficulty separating from his mother when he arrives at school. Finally he settles in at the puzzle (or small manipulatives) table with Elizabeth (teacher 1) and begins working on a geometric shape board. After fifteen minutes he briefly runs to Suzanne (teacher 2) at the crafts table. Immediately he runs back. He works with graduated cups and appears confused when two are left over. He begins building with unit cubes. He turns to me: 'See what I made!' I say, 'Tell me about it'. And he replies, 'It's a building'. Chris moves over to work with flat geometric shapes and sorts them into the Playskool caddy. After five minutes he leaves to paint at the easel. Roxanne (teacher 3) asks him which colors he wants and he responds 'the green and the blue one'. Shortly after, he returns to the puzzle table again to work on the geometric shape board. Although he has spent most of the morning here, he has sat in several different seats, moving to the materials rather than moving the materials to himself.

After about twenty minutes he leaves the table and moves to the block area. He rides a small tractor that had been in the corner. Seeing me, he says, 'I'm waiting for the man!' Then, 'I'm waiting for that boy. This is broken. The wheel doesn't turn.' I say, 'What should we do?' And he answers, 'We shouldn't play with it. It doesn't work.' (while seated on it.) 'How could we fix it?' I ask. 'It needs a new steering wheel. We should put it away.' At this he runs off, saying, 'I want to play with something'. He comes back riding a bus, then notices a child building and asks him what he is doing. He begins stacking blocks on top of the child's structure. This is the first time all morning that I have observed him interacting with another child, though, initially, he had stood on the child's foot to get his attention. 'See!' he

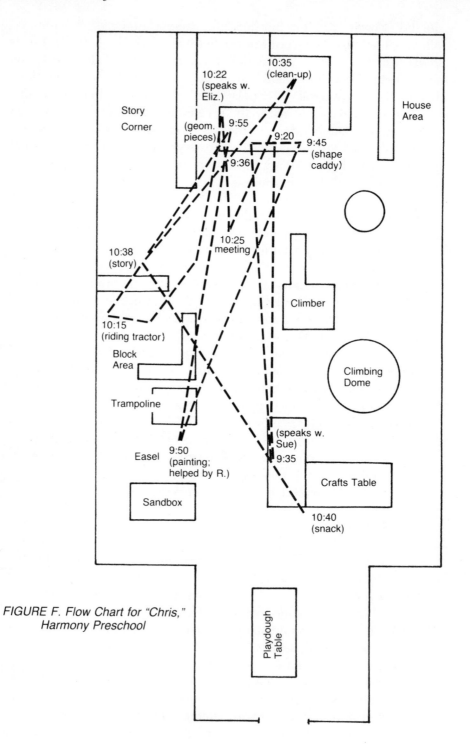

FIGURE F. Flow Chart for "Chris,"
Harmony Preschool

yells at me. I ask him if his row of blocks is the same length. He blinks briefly. 'Is it as long as the other one?' 'Yes,' he says, 'I am certain'.

After a brief time he runs again to Elizabeth, stopping on the way to chase another child. He repeatedly pushes his face into the other child's face, laughing antagonistically. 'I'm thirsty', he tells her. She answers, 'We will have snack very soon'. He briefly stands by Danny and watches him, though he directs his comments to Elizabeth. Then he begins working with the geometric board again. Shortly after, morning meeting is called. After roll is taken, clean-up time begins. He stands behind Elizabeth and watches what she does. He puts the lid on the box of colored bears, then helps to pick up the small bears on the floor. (Elizabeth points these out, and several children begin to crawl about for them.) In the process the pegboard pieces spill and Chris also helps pick up these. Only two children are left 'cleaning up.' Chris is now talking with Suzanne who is finishing the clean-up procedure at the puzzle table. Elizabeth has begun reading a story. Chris crawls through the shelf. Elizabeth reprimands: 'Chris, that's not a good place to be'. He returns to Suzanne and watches her close the toy shelf and lock it. At Suzanne's suggestion he moves next to Elizabeth for the story.

Chris moves through space in a somewhat circumscribed manner. Most of his time is spent at the puzzle table, with brief forays to the crafts table (only to say something to a teacher and then return), to the paint easel (for five minutes), and to the block area, where he rides a tractor, speaks with me, and briefly interacts with a child who is building. He spends most of his time in what has been characterized as 'parallel play'. His two interactions with children suggest that (i) he is in a 'mood' on this day, or (ii) he has not yet learned to get the attention of other children in a socially acceptable manner (i.e., he steps on one child's hand before speaking to him, chases the other to thrust his face into his). His comments are directed towards the adults in the room. He primarily works in an area where an adult is present and, during the transition time (clean-up to story), he carefully watches what the adult does and tries to do the same.

When I gave the head teacher copies of the 'flow charts' on the day following this observation, she was laughingly tolerant of Chris, explaining that he was, after all, 'still a babe', the only child of professional parents. He is usually with adults, she explained, and is 'deceptively verbal'.

Sue and Chris differ in their utilization of space and patterns of interaction, yet several generalizations can be made about the way in which they function in the classroom. First, both children have begun 'school' at an early age: Sue had begun the year before when she was three; Chris has just turned three. Second, both children spend this nearly one-and-a-half-hour block of time choosing activities in the room that are of interest to them. Their use of space is fluid, and they begin and end most activities with neither overt adult assistance nor interference. Third, both children freely (and primarily) interact with the adults in the setting. They initiate conversations with adults: 'I want to paint!' 'Look at my big ball!' 'See what I did!' 'I'm thirsty.' Both children appear to assume that adults are there (i) to praise them for their efforts and accomplishments; and (ii) to help them when they need assistance. Fourth, the children individuate by their selection of activities (interests). And, finally, much of the 'learning' that goes on is through implicit instruction. The children move into an area and apprehend that certain behaviors are appropriate there (one cuts at the crafts table, pours at the water table, rolls and pounds at the playdough table, etc.) The choices available to children are limited to primarily productive, action-oriented, transformational type activities that the teachers perceive as educational. In this sense, the child's very movement through space is considered to be an indication that he or she is learning what the teachers intend. When a child would sit for an extended time in one place, a teacher would attempt to entice that child into some form of productive activity. Yet I seldom observed a child just sitting. (See the discussion that follows regarding 'non-productive activity.') The environment is a kaleidoscope of activity, carefully structured to lure children from one space to another, from this interest to that.

At Irving Head Start the movement of children through space has a different rhythm and flow. After breakfast, 'free time' is characterized by the fact that children play freely, generally without adult interference. Thus, Sanford uses most of this time to run behind a large, wooden truck. He and several other boys map out a course, or, at least, appear to run over and over in the same general pattern.

He briefly climbs into the rocking boat where three other children sit; he smiles a lot and tells them something his 'mamma' said but then quickly returns to his truck. The teachers' view of this area from teacher space is blocked by a line of bulletin boards. Only when a child cries or complains or when the noise rises noticeably in pitch does a teacher venture into the back of the classroom.

Jeannine uses this 'free' time to play with six other girls in the house area. She arranges a cabinet, sweeps, cares for a 'baby' until clean-up

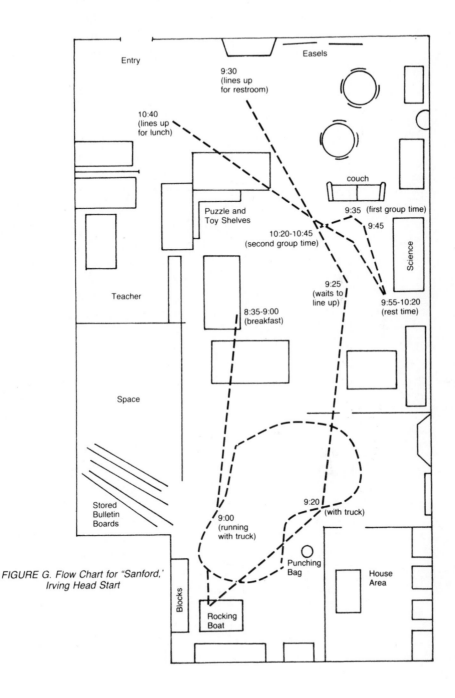

FIGURE G. Flow Chart for "Sanford,'
Irving Head Start

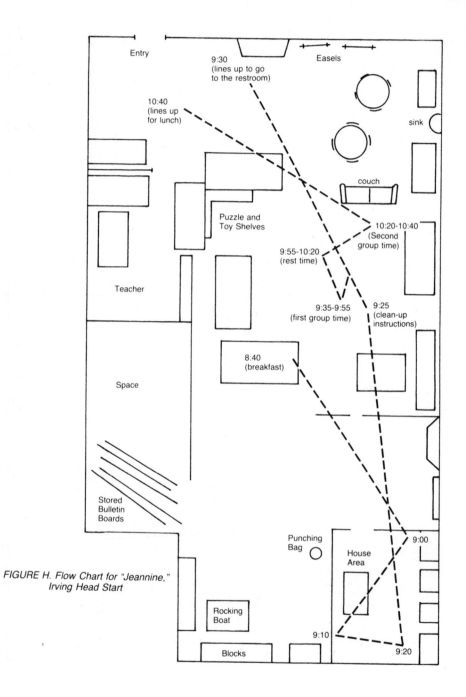

Entry

9:30
(lines up to go
to the restroom)

Easels

sink

10:40
(lines up
for lunch)

couch

Puzzle and
Toy Shelves

10:20-10:40
(Second
group time)

9:55-10:20
(rest time)

Teacher

9:35-9:55
(first group time)

9:25
(clean-up
instructions)

8:40
(breakfast)

Space

Stored
Bulletin
Boards

Punching
Bag

House
Area

9:00

FIGURE H. Flow Chart for "Jeannine,"
Irving Head Start

Rocking
Boat

9:10

9:20

Blocks

time is signalled by the dimming of the lights. During this time she doesn't speak.

The choices of activities on this day are two puzzles, trucks, a rocking boat, a punching bag and the dolls, utensils and furniture present in the house area. Most of the children are playing with things in the back of the room. Since blocks are available but located in the same area, on this day it is not possible to construct anything with them.

For the remainder of the morning Sanford and Jeannine use space in much the same way, because they are involved in group activities. They listen to the teacher, line up to go to the restrooms, return for group time, rest for twenty-five minutes and then have another group time. They line up again to go to cafeteria for lunch, and when they return they wait on the red rug until the van arrives to take them home.

Sanford is four years of age; Jeannine will be four shortly. Both children are in school for the first time. After breakfast, the children have a thirty-minute period of 'free play'. As is common in preschools everywhere, their selection of activities reflects their sex: Sanford plays with a truck and on a 'boat', Jeannine plays at housekeeping. During this time neither child speaks much, but, when they do, their comments are directed towards their peers. Neither child appears to be aware of — or in need of — the teachers, who are out of sight in another section of the room.

Autonomy/Authority

As Hall (1959, 1966 and 1977) has demonstrated, the use of space reflects cultural patterns of interpersonal interaction, and considerations of time and space are functionally interrelated. The preschool teachers share the space with the children, and few outside demands interrupt their time. For much of the morning, the children move through space with a certain degree of autonomy. The general atmosphere is informal, as evidenced by the fact that the children call the adults by their first names.

At the Head Start center the space appears to underscore the distinction between adults and children. It is divided into two areas: one in which the teachers attend to adult responsibilities, the other in which the children are provided breakfast, free play time and group instruction. The duties of the Head Start teachers are likewise clearly divided. Just as they must use time to deal with responsibilities extraneous to the children, so too space is provided wherein these tasks can be accomplished. The demands of the program are such that they are frequently interrupted, in which case they move from the children to the other duties or contrarily from the duties to the children.

But the separate space also provides a kind of retreat, a place where adults can have some privacy. The teachers both work full-time and have more diverse responsibilities both at work and at home. They are surrounded by children for seven hours while working and go home to more of the same. The ubiquitous nature and constancy of these demands seems to create a need to 'get away' and to 'be away' for some portion of each day. 'Free space,' like 'free time,' means something quite different in each setting.

In most time frames, the children are expected to occupy the same space as others. As in many traditional societies, the teachers believe that children learn from adults who are invested with greater knowledge and wisdom. Thus, the children spend much of their time grouped with other children or gathered around one of the teachers for group instruction. Such practices would seem to reinforce the communality of experience among group members, as well as to stress the importance of authority. In the Head Start center teachers are called by their last names.[2]

Notes

1 The head teacher at the Head Start Center left at the end of September and was replaced by a teacher who remained until the end of the year. Early in October the teachers moved the couch to the back of 'teacher space.' Other changes were made at that time, for example, the large trucks were put away, and the block area was moved. These spatial changes remained for the duration of the school year. Figure D represents this utilization of space; figures G and H reflect the early usage.

2 The head teacher was always concerned that the children called me by my first name and said she would have never allowed it had she been there from the first of the year. She thought that, because of this, the children didn't see me as an authority figure. I tried to reassure her. 'You know, it's different in different places. At the Harmony Preschool and at Child-school children call the teachers by their first names.' She had raised an eyebrow and suggested that those places probably had nothing but trouble.

7   *Activities and Materials*

Just as people organize time and space to achieve valued ends, so, too, are materials arranged and utilized in a purposeful (if unconscious) manner. Following the descriptions of a 'typical' day in each setting, beliefs and practices regarding the use of material objects are analyzed in terms of the nature and purpose of the curriculum. Generalizations are then made about the nature of the children, the nature of the behavior expected and valued and the nature of materials in the respective settings.

The preschool children are shown to be in an environment where progressive change both through multiplicity and differentiation is experienced as positive and where individualism is desirable. Children are encouraged to be active and to produce divergent responses through the manipulation of transformational materials. The center children are shown to be in an environment where static (social) knowledge is valued, where group consensus and convergent response are expected, and where the orientation is to the repeated act rather than to change. Children are encouraged to attend to what the adult says during much of their school time, and the use of materials is considered less important.

The Preschool

Outside there is the gentlest of rains. It falls like mist on the boulevard and merges with the grass like dew. One by one children and their mothers slip through the entry hall, now cluttered with umbrellas and rubber boots. The clamor and echo in the hall contrast with the hum of activity inside the classroom, where children are already busy with the day's activities.

A large, banana-shaped sign, painted bright yellow, still hangs on the classroom door: 'Next week is fruit week. Would everyone please bring one fruit each.' A large crystal fruit bowl sits on the first table as one enters. It contains a pineapple, a bunch of grapes, two oranges and an apple. Elizabeth sits at this table painting Jennifer's fingernails red. Sandra and Jimmy are watching. Chris and several others move over to have their nails painted as well. Elizabeth asks Jennifer how many nails are red, then paints a '5' on the back of her hand.

Suzanne is at the crafts table making pink playdough with nine children. 'What do you suppose will happen', she queries, 'if we add red food coloring?' Markets and paper are available on the table that intersects with the crafts table, where Suzanne is working. The water table has been set up in the room this week. A 'Rub Goldberg' machine sits in the water. Wheels turn when water is poured over them. Roxanne approaches a child, 'Dan, I have red paint at the easel today. Would you like to paint a red picture?'

No manipulatives are out, though Suzanne later places two puzzles on this table. After making dough she leaves the table and goes behind the house area to pull out 'dress-ups' for children. She hopes to encourage a more dramatic use of the house area. Jim works near her, alternatively playing with the Tumble Tower and building with bristle blocks.

Several boys play 'Luke Skywalker and Darth Vader' around the climbing dome most of the morning. As Dave begins flying ships around the room, Elizabeth rises to invite him to her table: 'Dave, I'm painting everyone's fingernails red. Would you like me to paint your fingernails red?' Dave declines. 'O.K., let me see if Adam would like to come.' Dave runs off to get Charles: 'Come on, let's pretend I'm Luke Skywalker.' As the boys re-enact and improvize 'Star Wars,' climbing the dome, flying ships, playing dead, the classroom activities continue around them.

After one hour and thirty minutes a bell is rung. The children gather on the floor for 'meeting'. When all are seated, Elizabeth says: 'Some of you chose to have red fingernails today. Look what we have on our bulletin board. What is it?' Children say, 'A red balloon.' 'And look what else we have!' She pulls a partially blown balloon from behind her back. 'Some balloons fly if they have a special gas in them. It's called helium. How can I make this one move?' One child yells, 'Let it go!' She releases it, and it skitters across the room. 'The air came out so fast that it pushed the balloon across the room.' Roxanne then demonstrates how a balloon can make music. Then Suzanne says, 'But did you know that balloons are quite dangerous? If the balloon went in your mouth you couldn't get air to breathe.' Elizabeth concurs, 'That's right. You should let your mommy or daddy blow up balloons for you. Do you know what time it is now?' Several children holler, 'Clean up!'

After the room has been straightened, the children reconvene, this time in the book area. After reprimanding a child, Elizabeth gets everyone's attention: 'Boys and girls, now it's time to listen. Please put your books away. Some people brought some fruit today. Don't tell me if you did or didn't. If you did, we're very glad, and if you didn't, then you can bring something later this week.' She shows the children the pineapple, asks what it is, then asks for words to describe a pineapple. The children offer brown, round ... 'And how does it feel?' 'Prickly.' 'Oh, yes, it's quite prickly. I'm going to pass it round so that everyone can feel how prickly it is.' Elizabeth then reads a story. The children have fresh pineaple chunks and water for snack. Small groups meet briefly, then there is music time as mothers arrive.

The Center

In the early morning, a good hour before the local elementary school will commence classes, the blue and gold van meanders in and out of streets, stopping occasionally to wait for a child to bound out of house or apartment. It is a fine fall morning. Leaves have begun to turn; there is a briskness and clarity to the air. From start to finish the ride takes approximately forty-five minutes. About 8.30 a.m. the children tumble from the van and race across the parking lot. Miss Washington, the aide, waits for them at the door and escorts them to the room, where Mrs. Barker, the head teacher, is busy setting the tables for breakfast. The children scramble onto seats and wait.

The morning's fare of juice and cereal comes pre-packaged in individual containers. The small cereal boxes are stored in the locked cabinet in the teachers' area. Milk and juice are kept in the refrigerator in the classroom. Though the meal is simple, it takes time to distribute napkins, bowls, spoons, straws, juice and cereal. Then the teachers must help children open the boxes. The phone rings, and one teacher is left to finish. Most of the children eat quietly, though there is some talking, some grinning. 'Miss Washington, Sharron took my spoon.' The teacher chooses not to deal with this so early in the morning. She hands the child another spoon and walks away.

One by one the children finish and move to the red rug, where they wait for the other children to finish. Shortly before 9.00 a.m. Mrs. Barker clears away the last of the styrofoam bowls and crumpled napkins. She sits on a chair above the children and begins to assign them to different areas in the room: four to the library area, nine to the puzzle area, three to the housekeeping area, two to blocks. The children may not leave their assigned spaces. Approximately twenty-five minutes later clean-up time is signalled as the lights in the classroom are turned off. Children are expected to help clean up in the dim, indirect light from the windows.

After returning from the restrooms, the children have a twenty-five-minute group time. Mrs. Barker does a lesson on cucumbers. She cuts one and gives a slice to each child. 'This is a cucumber. What is this inside?' There is no response. 'We had some on the table. We talked about it last week.' Again, there is no response. 'They are called seeds. A cucumber is a relative of a pickle. Are pickles sour or sweet? ... A pickle is something that's sour, but we have sweet pickles, too. We like to eat them on our hamburger with a big ol' piece of onion.' Mrs. Barker takes roll, while Miss Washington gets a set of alphabet cards ready. Miss Washington then takes over. She explains that she wants all the children to learn to write their names or at least learn to recognize them. 'We use letters to name things and numbers to count things. But we're not talking about numbers today, are we?' She holds up letter cards, one at a time and asks individual children to recognize them. 'Raise your hand if you know it. Repeat after me: This is an "F". At the end of the activity, rest time is called. The children rest on blankets, mats and sheets on the floor. Two lie on the red rug. After thirty minutes, they put their bedding away and line up for the trip to the cafeteria for lunch. Children eat quietly in the large, basement cafeteria. As other classes begin to arrive, they file back to their room to wait on the red rug until it is time for the van to arrive.

The above descriptions of two days, one at the Harmony Preschool and one at the Irving Head Start Center, are not atypical. Moreover, an inductive analysis of each characterizes some of the differences between them, particularly as it informs the selection of activities and use of materials in each setting. The differences can perhaps best be seen in table form.

Table 1:   *Dimensions of Differences: Harmony and Irving Head Start*

	Harmony	**Irving Head Start**
Nature of the Curriculum	linear	repetitive
Purpose of the Curriculum (focus)	individuation multiplicity differentiation	group consensus
	orientation to change	orientation to the repeated act
Nature of Children	active	quiet and attentive
Nature of Behavior Expected and Valued	divergent response	convergent response
Nature of Materials	transformational	static
	highly organized (differentiated)	

Nature of the Curriculum

As previously explained, the Harmony teachers have a year-long plan, that, though modified, nonetheless provides them with a linear conception of the year's activities. This day represents one point in time. It is a day during 'fruit week,' the week children will have the opportunity to think about the abstraction 'fruit' by experiencing numerous examples: a pineapple, grapes, apples, oranges, etc. It is also 'red' week, which 'fits into' the broader category of color. After the eight weeks children spend exploring of color in many different contexts, their understanding of color is expected to be vastly expanded. The linear curriculum is consonant with the teachers' operating assumption that children 'develop', that 'growth' is characterized by increasing skill and language through the differentiation of experience.

By contrast, many of the activities at the Center are repeated from one day to the next. There is less mobility among areas and less change within them. Activities are somewhat compartmentalized, just as the day itself is cut up into various tasks that need to be done each and every day. There is little relation between and among them. Children do what they are assigned or expected to do in each time frame. Though the children can decide what to do within the area to which they are assigned, the choices are more limited than at the preschool and the time allotted shorter.

At group time Beverly shows the children a cucumber, asks what is inside. Though 'some were on the table. We talked about them last week,' the children do not respond to the hints provided. Likewise the distinctions between a cucumber and a pickle and between sweet and sour seem less clear, though, interestingly, the teacher says that the cucumber is 'a relative' of a pickle, suggesting that the important characteristic for her is the similarity. This was the only time during the year, save for holiday parties, in which the head teacher brought food into the classroom.

Group time ends as Miss Washington flashes alphabet cards the children are to recognize. Although this activity is done for one day only, immediately after this name cards were made and several days each week children were asked to recognize their names. Repetition of forms is considered to be a learning experience that simulates the learning of later schooling and is different than 'just playing'.

Purpose of the Curriculum

At Harmony an attempt is made to create a curriculum that focuses on the increasing differentiation of experience through sensory experience and through language. The head teacher believes that the purpose of the curriculum is to help children to become individuals who are both self-motivated and distinct, one from another.

On this day children have the opportunity to experience red objects in a variety of forms. Their fingernails are painted red; they can add red food coloring to white playdough to make 'pink' playdough; they can paint a red picture; they watch a red balloon zip through the air. They also see, feel and taste a pineapple.

Through a multiplicity of experiences abstractions are variously conceived. The abstraction 'number' becomes five painted fingers which a child can count. The '5' on his or her hand represents the counting. And red is not a color on a flash card but rather, in the words of Mary O'Neill's well-known adventure in color:

Red is an Indian,
A Valentine heart,
The trimmings on

A circus cart
Red is lipstick
Red is a shout
Red is a signal
That says 'Watch out!'
Red is a great big
Rubber ball.
Red is the giant-est
Color of all.

It would seem that such experiences in context and over time would help children to classify a range of objects and events within broader abstract categories.

Finally, the environment is constantly changing, but in subtle ways that the children themselves can discover. Fruit is here and was not before. It is on a table and can be touched; later one kind will be eaten. Fingernails are painted. The water table has been set up this week; a 'Rub Goldberg' machine is there. Red paint, for the first time, is at the easel. And Suzanne is getting out 'dress-up' — another new experience for the children.

Many of these activities require new behaviors. In the context of the classroom, language is a commonly encouraged means of defining experience. We 'paint' pictures, but we also 'paint' fingernails. A balloon will fly if it is filled with 'helium', or, if we just 'let it go', 'air pushes a balloon across the room'. Pineapples are brown and round to look at and 'prickly' to feel and sweet to taste.

These children come from families who likewise value (and can afford) a multiplicity of experiences. These are children who will be offered cello lessons, taken to the beach for summer vacation, helped to build model airplanes, taken to the library. To this end, the school both reinforces and extends the familiar home environment.

The overriding assumption that governs much of the classroom activity is that children are unique and that further individuation is desirable. Children are offered a range of activities: they are allowed to *choose* the ones that interest them, to decline an invitation to join an activity that does not. It is believed that the task a child chooses is inherently motivating and that, unlike structured group activities, it is more than likely developmentally appropriate for the child. Thus, Dave can decline to have his fingernails painted and continue his preferred pretend play as 'Luke Skywalker'.

Language is encouraged as a means of differentiating one's experience from — and conveying it to — others. But other forms of production (painting, drawing, crafts) are also encouraged as a means of expressing unique experience. Teachers 'keep track of' children by scanning the bulletin boards each day to see who has and has not done certain kinds of productive work. The materials available (paint, markers, playdough) encourage *divergent* responses. There are no coloring books or ditto sheets in the room. Children are not given ducks to color yellow or trees to color green, nor do they make uniform hats, snowmen or ashtrays. Unique response is considered a desirable goal.

Beyond the teachers' vigilance and encouragement, however, the bulletin boards appear to serve another function. They provide the children themselves with a bit of individual space, a place for 'my things and no one else's'. Just as children frequently initiate interaction with a teacher ('Look at me!' 'Look what I made!') the board space provides a place for a non-verbal display of individuality. At the end of the morning this is often the first place where mother and child go together, either at the mother's initiative ('Show me what you did in school today'.) or at the child's ('Come see what I made, mommy!'). In diverse ways such as these individuation is encouraged.

At the Center the teachers are busy feeding, cleaning, storing, keeping records, maintaining communication with parents and superiors by telephone, etc. Far less time is available for instruction per se. Unlike the focus on the individual that appears to characterize the preschool, children eat as a group, are assigned to areas in groups; they convene for an extended 'group time', ,rest as a group, eat lunch as a group. They also spend time 'waiting' as a group, for no one is allowed to proceed to the activity in the next time frame until all are ready to do so. Thus, children wait before group time, wait in line to go to the restrooms and to the cafeteria, wait for the van to arrive. In subtle ways such as these children appear to be conditioned to conform to the expectations for the group.

Children are instructed through the repetition of forms, expected to recognize rather than reconstruct. Individualism is, in fact, frequently perceived as 'deviance'. The child who speaks out of turn, who does not conform, receives negative attention. Language is frequently taught by rote: 'Repeat after me. This is an "F."' Finally, children hang their coats or jackets on any hooks that are available and are not assigned individual spaces.

Going beyond the two days described above, several generalizations can be made regarding the nature of children, the nature of behavior expected and valued, and the nature of the materials offered in the two settings.

The Nature of Children

The Harmony classroom is highly differentiated; ten to twelve activity areas are available to children at any given time. And the preschool children are encouraged to be active — to move from space to space.

Table 2:   *Activity Areas at Harmony and Irving*

Activity Centers	
Harmony Pre-school	*Irving Head Start*
sand	
water	water table (filled occasionally at year's end)
playdough	several times before Christmas
markers, crayons and paper	
blocks	blocks
climbing dome	
jungle gym (bars and slide)	
book area	library area
house area	'housekeeping'
'puzzle' table	puzzle area
easels used everyday	easels (used once a month/first three months)
science table	science table
music (floor used; no separate area)	music area
park	school playground (for most of the year no outdoor play)

Group time offers still more variety: a new story each day (books are borrowed regularly from the local public library), a frequent change of fare at snack time, possibly small group activity and music in short frames of time, and another free time period at the neighborhood park, where swings, slides, seesaws and tunnels are available.

Head Start children have about twenty-five minutes per day for free time. They are assigned generally to one of *four* areas: blocks, house-keeping, puzzles, library. Approximately one hour each day is spent eating breakfast and lunch, another thirty minutes is allowed for resting, and about thirty minutes for group time, a period of time in which children have some kind of academic instruction (counting, name recognition, learning birthdays, addresses and phone numbers, learning about the calendar) and/or listen to music. The Head Start children are expected to conform more tightly to scheduled events, to eat when the group eats, to play where assigned, to go to the restrooms as a group, to sit quietly during group time and lie quietly during rest time. Thus, children are expected to be quiet and attentive and to wait to be told what to do for much of the school day.

The Nature of Behavior Expected and Valued

Different kinds of behavior seem to be expected of the children, that is, they are expected to react to the materials and activities in different ways in the respective settings. Though many of the materials at Harmony (particularly at the puzzle table which contains a wide variety of small manipulatives) require that the child do them correctly, the materials themselves tend to be self-correcting. A puzzle can be done one way only, and, if a child does not put the graduated cylinders in the correct holes he or she will have one or two left over. A teacher is usually present to offer assistance or to select a manipulative that is 'developmentally appropriate.' But the materials are such that the teacher generally does not need to direct a child how to use them.

The many transformational materials on the other hand, appear to foster *divergent* responses. The children seem to apprehend that divergent responses gain them recognition in the eyes of adults. Thus, there are plum pie and bird's nests made of playdough, a dinosaur painted at the easel, etc. The nature of the materials enables and encourages children to continuously construct and reconstruct new things — things which distinguish them from one another.

At the Center the teachers are not available during free time, so there generally is no adult to acknowledge the fact that a child has completed something. Art projects tend to be done as a group. All the pumpkin men at Halloween looked just alike. For Thanksgiving children were shown how to paste Indian feathers, previously cut out by the aide, onto a construction paper band. All of the girls had three feathers: all of the boys had one each. At Christmas, all the dittoed gingerbread men were brown. Later, all the children colored a ditto of Martin Luther King brown. At Easter all of the chicks had to be yellow. In this sense, as in teacher-student interaction generally, there was great value placed on *convergent* responses. Generally, a child who didn't do something as he/she was told simply did it wrong.

The Nature of Materials

Materials at Harmony tend to be transformational in nature, enabling children to act on objects and to 'construct continuities over time'

(Forman and Kuschner, 1978). Sand, water, playdough, clay, markers, blocks and paint are all materials that can be utilized and structured in many different ways. Children can use the same material (for example, sand) to make tunnels, cakes, roads, etc. The material thus takes on the characteristics which the child gives it.

The material can also be changed prior to the children's use of it in order to foster new possibilities. The sand is wet some weeks, dry others. A variety of buckets, shovels, spoons, sifters, trucks and cars are provided. Water is soapy or clear. The water table contains measuring cups, pitchers, cups, whisks, or a 'Rub Goldberg' machine. Playdough is made by teacher and children nearly every week and dyed a different color. At the playdough table I heard teachers and children discuss cakes and pies (chocolate cake, lemon meringue pie, etc.), peas, islands, people, snowmen, spirals and cups. At the crafts table at various times children learned to make collages, montages, fringe, necklaces, etc. Blocks, likewise, offer children endless opportunities for constructing roads, buildings, enclosures, bridges, gates, etc. However, the teachers work this area infrequently, generally allowing children (usually boys) to construct on their own. Finally the color of the paint changes from week to week at the easels. Colors that would mix with the 'color of the week' are often available. Thus, a child is able to discover that yellow and red make orange or that blue and red make purple without any direct teacher instruction (see the discussion that follow on the nature of interaction). Things appear to be valued less in the Head Start classroom and were considered less useful.

The Head Start teachers see the materials in the room as play-things to keep children occupied before instruction begins. Blocks are the only transformational material available every day. Three other areas are used regularly during free time. In the library area there is a core of books that were on the shelves for the entire year. The puzzle area had the same shelf collection for the first three months of school and then changed only slightly. The housekeeping area, likewise, had the same materials and ethos all year. Thus, the materials tend to remain the same and generally are not transformational in nature.

Finally, materials at Harmony, like the curriculum, are highly organized. Blocks are carefully shelved according to shape and size. In the house area there is a small tray of aluminium cutlery: there are plates, cups, saucers, a teapot, coffee pot, sugar bowl and creamer. There are pots and pans and even a skillet.

At the Center the organization of materials appears to be less important. Blocks are frequently thrown on shelves at clean-up time. A table near the science table holds a collection of large plastic animals.

There is a lion, a camel, an elephant, a zebra — and a cow.

Generally, children work with puzzles and materials alone. If they cannot do a puzzle after trying, it is often left on the table. Rubber cards numbered from 1–10 with pegs are also on the shelves. Only once did I observe a child seriate them sequentially and proceed to put the correct number of pegs in each. Children would use them randomly: a 5 card, an 8 card, a 2, a 4. Often the correct number of pegs were not inserted in the holes. Thus, it was doubtful that this material actually would help children to comprehend the concept of number and its relation to a set number of things.

All this suggests that materials and activities serve different ends in the two classrooms. Abstraction through language and experience and the ordering of experience into discrete categories are important for the Harmony teachers, and less so for the Head Start teachers, who tend to teach social knowledge through verbal interaction. One of the evolving themes developed in this research is that the Head Start teachers seem to place more stock in what is said than in what is written; they attend more to group needs than to individual needs, and they value peer interaction more than individualism. In this important sense, they attend to and re-create values which are more akin to traditional African cultures than to the individualistic, achievement-oriented norms of the industrialized West.

Object-oriented/Person-oriented

The use of materials and structuring of activities, like the utilization of time and space, appear to serve different purposes in the respective settings. Whereas the preschool teachers see the curriculum as a linear progressive that stimulates the linear development (growth) of the children, the Head Start teachers establish a curriculum that is repeated day after day. And while the preschool teachers stress individuation through multiplicity and differentiation, orienting children to expect, value and even control change through the manipulation of every-changing materials, the Head Start teachers stress consensus (the one right answer), social bonding (stressing equality among members), and an orientation both to authority and to the repeated act.

In each setting, however, children are encouraged to focus on different aspects of their environment. Based on fieldwork in a southern Georgia community, Young (1970) has made an important distinction between the White and Black child rearing practices which she observed. White parents provided their children with many toys which they were encouraged to manipulate. Black parents, by contrast, neither valued nor encouraged play with things. Rather children's attention appeared repeatedly to be focused on people.

Such a difference was likewise observable in the two settings described here. At the preschool the teachers believe that their primary responsibility lay in providing activities and materials, developing both the children's ability to manipulate these materials and their facility with language. Thus the space is filled with 'interesting things', and the teachers encourage and reward (with attention) the children's efforts.

There is a strong emphasis on transformational materials (paint, sand, water, clay, blocks) which both allow children to make unique constructions and which likewise reinforce the changing nature of things. Much of the language that transpires in the classroom is related to what the child has done to such materials ('Look at my big ball!' 'It's a nest'), further providing opportunities through which a child can distinguish his/her activity from that of others.

At the Head Start Center the overall space changes little over time; materials remain the same and transformational materials are provided infrequently. For example, the art easels were only in use once during the first three months; sand was never available; the water table was set up late in April. And the aquarium with a plastic turtle bubbled away on the science table for the entire year but never served any instructional purpose. For the Head-Start teachers teaching and learning have little to do with such things. Instead instruction focuses on social knowledge that can be transferred verbally from adult to child.

At this point one can only speculate how the world comes to children variously socialized. Perhaps the child who is socialized in a linear fashion can more readily adapt to the sequential mode of elementary school instruction, where a variety of subjects are explored in 'units' that interrelate over time. Or perhaps, as Talbert (1971) suggests, children who are accustomed to instigating interaction with adults are more likely to do well in American schools. The nature of interaction in the respective settings will be the focus the topic of the next section.

8   *Patterns of Interaction*

Throughout recorded history the young of every tribe, group and nation have learned what was needed to survive and to become social beings. Yet in contemporary times there is a tendency to see education as place specific (children learn in school) and knowledge specific (children must learn certain specified skills and facts). What this view abrogates is the vast amount of learning children bring to school. As Wax and Wax (1971) have pointed out, we tend to take it as unproblematic that children are pupils, but we ignore the process by which children become pupils.

As has been demonstrated, this process is quite complex, orienting children in time and in space, directing them to use certain artifacts in specified ways, encouraging them to learn from others in social situations or to impose their own order onto objects and events through the manipulation of things. Education is more than simply a process of learning skills; it is also the process of being incorporated into an ongoing tradition.

Much of this process is mediated through interaction with adults and with peers. As the present study has demonstrated the nature of the relationship between adults and children is different in the respective settings. Learning in the preschool is perceived as a largely interactive process between adults and children. What ultimately appears to be mediated is the relationship between immediate experiences and more formalized abstractions such as color, shape and number. Verbal interaction (communication) with adults becomes for children a means of thinking about what they are doing. Learning in the center maintains the distinction between immediate experience (the children play alone) and abstract social knowledge (the formalized group time) and the link between them is less obvious.

The introduction of the present section relates classroom patterns to larger social contexts. The chapter attempts to demonstrate how, in these early education settings, classroom practices are consonant with children's home experiences. Interaction is defined as the meaningful action that takes place between and among people. Interaction patterns between adults and children are then analyzed in each setting.

Introduction

The Harmony teachers are white, middle-class Protestants in a nation that is highly technological and industrialized. They value change and individualism as is evident in their espousal of 'personal growth' and 'development' and 'individual achievement'. Yet this valuing is also evident in the transformational materials they provide and in their encouragement of individual 'products' and increasingly differentiated vocabularies. The 'bright' child distinguishes himself or herself from others, and 'good' teaching fosters precisely that.

But this is somehow not surprising. For, in middle-class America, separation and individuation are encouraged from an early age. A young child sleeps alone, is frequently weaned early. Nuclear families move about and often live hundreds of miles from extended families. In a rapidly changing society satisfaction comes from *personal* growth and achievement rather than from a sense of community and oneness with others (Kluckhohn and Kluckhohn, 1947).

Within the limits defined by society individuals believe they have 'freedom' or free choice. They select the mode of dress that will characterize their identities, select the type of housing they prefer, the professions they will enter, the moral code they will espouse, the church they will attend or not attend. And, early on, a preschool likewise offers the young a smorgasbord of activities and choices.

What is observable in this preschool ultimately is the socialization of children into the pre-eminent values of the society, values which the teachers themselves have internalized. The values have become, as Schutz has stated, 'the world-taken-for-granted'.

In the Head Start center one sees not merely the inverse of trends and patterns evident in the preschool, but rather a quite different moral order. The Head Start teachers are Black, and, though they can be said to be neither 'poor' nor 'uneducated', their values and behavior have been mediated by the Black experience in America. In the face of racial prejudice and rampant inequality, Blacks appear to have a concept of kinship quite alien to the more stereotypic ideas of individualistic America. The teachers are concerned with group solidarity, and there is less room for individuality, for, intuitively, the concept itself is divisive. The 'bright' child functions well within the classroom setting, is able to converge on the correct answer to the teacher's questions, and 'good' teaching fosters the ability to do that.

From an early age, a Black child is likely to live in an extended family, with grandparents, aunts, uncles or cousins, as well as siblings, likely, as people move in and out with changing circumstances, to have a broadened sense of 'family'. A Black child is far more likely to sleep with others, to experience less privacy (and also less loneliness) than a White American child. A child will frequently be nurtured and supervised by more than one primary adult. And, very often, older siblings, even those only a few years older, will have significant child-care responsibilities.

The Black experience ultimately reflects a dynamic and functional response to racial prejudice in all its subtlety. To a large extent poor Black Americans survive through kinship networks. And children are perhaps given a limited amount of choice because that is what Blacks have experienced historically. And so, children are enculturated in complex ways, not immediately apparent, to adapt to a different 'world-taken-for-granted'.

In the Center, the classroom environment is more peer-oriented than child-oriented. As the extended family is re-created in the classroom, children are well-supervised, but the teachers must also attend to other diffuse and manifold responsibilities. There is a great deal of support both in action and in words among the teachers for one another. Unlike the White preschool teachers who concentrate mainly on the children, who infrequently speak with one another (except as regards the children), there is a comraderie, an omnipresent 'together-ness', as tasks are shared, and stories, complaints, opinions, and humor freely aired. Children learn by repeating after the teacher, but they also learn that they are eminently social beings. Most of their classroom time is spent in the company of other children, either interacting among themselves or attending as a group to what the teacher has to say. These cultural patterns are learned early. They are part of the repertoire of behaviors that a child brings to early schooling, and they likewise reflect the previous socialization of the adults who organize the children's experience of school.

Interaction Between and Among Adults and Children

Interaction implies the exchange of meaning in two directions. In the sections that follow, the teachers' interactions with children, their actions and reactions, as well as the actions and reactions of the children will be investigated.

Interaction at Harmony: Teacher to Child

At the Harmony preschool adults and children interact frequently with one another, and time, space, and activity are constructed so as to foster such interactions. The teachers value productivity and individualism and, in daily practices that are consonant with these values, they encourage children to think and work divergently, to differentiate their experience from others, to be distinct one from the other. Much of the verbal interaction that transpires in the classroom relates to what the child has done or can do to objects. Since the objects in the classroom are in flux, new words are constantly needed to describe an ever-changing environment. Secondarily, verbal interaction serves to modulate choice. Different levels of intensity in the verbal messages used by adults require children to decode what is being encouraged or allowed, to judge or to discern their degree of freedom in a given situation. The discussion that follows, therefore, will elaborate on each of these topics in turn: the encouragement of productivity and individuality, language learning through the explication and differentiation of experience (i.e., the development of a 'particularized' vocabulary), the modulation of choice, and interactive failure: the 'problem child.'

The encouragement of productivity and individuality

During the period of observation the Harmony teachers spent most of their time with the children. They were physically with them and most of their comments, questions, and problems were child-directed. Occasional comments, notable for their brevity, were directed at another adult, but these generally dealt with functional matters related to the children or to the classroom.

The teachers exert a good deal of energy and imagination in individualizing instruction. There is an emphasis on what the individual child can do and a desire to see all children happy and productive. A brief excerpt from a transcript of Elizabeth at the puzzle table, who, on this day, seems atypically directive:

> 'That's a triangle, but it's too big. Put it there. That's it. You got it. That's the right place. Where does this go? That's a diamond shape. Try it here. Chris, let me help you with the house puzzle, 'cause I can tell that you have trouble with it.' [Elizabeth puts it together as Chris goes to get another puzzle from the shelf.] 'Chris, why don't you take it right over here. There's a little more room. Sue, did you get a chance to finish it? Good.'

Though teachers will sometimes have a specific activity in mind, conformity to one way of doing it is not demanded so long as the children appear to be working.

> Elizabeth is at the playdough table. It is orange this week. She has drawn a spiral on paper and is showing children how to roll the dough into a 'snake' and 'coil it' into a 'spiral.' Sandra throws a large gob onto the table. George is playing with a thick, hotdog-shaped piece. Sue is working with some rather shapeless pieces and stencils. Erin sits with a spiral Elizabeth had made in front of her. Only Joseph experiments with rolling a snake, then picks up a dull knife and begins cutting. Elizabeth leaves the table to help briefly in the kitchen.

On occasion a child will not be engaged in any kind of action or interaction. Non-productive behavior seems to call the teachers to action.

> Steve is lying on the floor. Elizabeth turns to me: 'I don't know how much longer I can let this continue.' She walks over to him. 'It's time for you to do some drawing.' She takes him by the hand and leads him to the table as she speaks.

As suggested above, children are commonly addressed by name ('Chris, why don't you take it right over there.' 'Sue, did you get a chance to finish it?') Children are also encouraged to call one another by name. At snack time, early in the year, Elizabeth addresses her group of 'older' children:

> 'You know what? I'm going to go all around our group, and you see if you know the names.' She walks behind each child and holds his or her head between her two hands while the children call out each child's name in turn. 'Is there anyone who could walk around and tell everyone's name?' Several children emulate her in turn. She asks if anyone else wants a turn, then tells them that 'we can do it again tomorrow'.

The overriding assumption is that a group is composed of individual members, that 'wholes' break into 'parts'.

Teachers also tell individual children how a change of behavior will benefit them individually.

> 'David, if you put your bottom down, then you will be able to see.'

> 'Ellen, go back by _____. You'll be able to see the picture so much better.'

115

Conformity to the teacher's suggestion thus frequently is invoked less from group norms than from individual benefit. Yet, on other occasions, explanations do refer to the needs of others:

> Sue, put this puzzle away if you're finished, so there's room for someone else to come.

Even here, however, the child is addressed as an individual, given a choice ('if you're finished'), and given an explanation for the reasonableness of the action.

The explication and differentiation of experience

Language becomes an important means of encouraging children to understand in their own terms what is going on. This serves not only to indicate to children what they are doing or hope to do, but also to inform the children of what the teachers are doing. The teachers seem to want the children to understand what is happening to them.

> Elizabeth helps two children at the easel. 'Would you like to do a picture, Rebecca? I'll put some paper on the other side for you. This one is for Laura Ellen. Here's the smock. The hole goes over your head and the straps go around in front. Rebecca, I ran out of paper. I'll go to the cupboard to get some more.'

A small group prepares to make playdough with Suzanne. Their interchange is typical of the individuation, verbal explanation and problem solving that is a common occurrence in the classroom.

> Suzanne sets a bag of flour on the table. 'What is this stuff?' (No response.) 'Is it sand?' 'No.' 'Butter?' 'No.' 'Milk?' 'No.' 'Flour?' Some nos, but some yesses. 'Yes, this is flour. What can we use it for?' One child: 'For bread.' *Another*: 'And cookies.' *Suzanne*: 'Yes. We can also use it to make playdough. Charles, do you want to help us make playdough?' *Adam* (yells): 'I do! But I'll have to wash my hands.' She hands the bag of flour to a child. 'Would you like to pour it in? Here, you can do it again.' *Another* (yells,): 'I want to help, too!' *Suzanne* asks: 'What is this stuff?' 'Salt.' 'Yes, this is salt. Andrea, would you like to sit in that seat over there? You'll be closer. I put the cup here so we can measure. Andrea, would you like to put the salt in the bowl?' *Andrea* asks what is in the bowl. *Suzanne* responds: 'It's called flour. Do you know what you can make with it?' 'Cake?' 'Yes, and you're making playdough with it. It came out of this bag. See the oil, Rebecca? Adam, can you put the oil in? I'm going to

116

make a little well. What color is that bottle? (I don't hear the response.) *Andrea to Adam*: 'Can I do it now?' *Suzanne*: 'Now let me pour just a wee bit more oil. What color will our playdough be?' *Adam*: 'Red.' 'Will it be red or something a little bit lighter?' *Adam*: 'Something a little bit lighter.' 'What color would that be?' Another child yells 'Salt!' Suzanne grimaces. *Sandra* runs up to her: 'Why are you doing that?' 'So we can have playdough for our school . . . like we had on Friday.' (To me: 'But Friday's wasn't good. It was too stiff.') Suzanne divides the ball of playdough into glumps and hands them to the children. *Adam* runs up to her: 'I have to wash my hands. I was playing in the sandbox again.' Shortly after, he announces: 'I'm spilling flour.' *Andrea:* 'I'm spilling it on my dress and on the floor.'
Sandra: 'I'm making a dinosaur.'
Another: 'I'm making an island.'
Suzanne: 'What is an island? What's it made of?'
Adam: 'Dirt.'
Suzanne: 'What's all around an island?'
David: 'Trees.'
Suzanne: 'How do you get there?'
David: 'By streets.'
Suzanne: 'Is it possible to get there on a ship?'
David: 'Yes, it's possible.'
Suzanne: 'It might be fun to make an island in the sandbox and pour water all around it to make an ocean.'
Adam: 'I'm making an island.'
Suzanne: 'And what's all around it?'
Adam: 'Roads.'
Andrea tells Suzanne that she needs some more dough.
Suzanne begins to sprinkle flour on the table: 'This is flour. What is this like?' (No answer.) 'You've all forgotten what happened last winter. It's like snow.' A conversation ensues among the children:
Jennifer: 'Last winter it snowed, and Santa Claus gave us presents, right?'
Sandra: 'And we got presents.'
Andrea: 'My grandmother was at my house.'
Sue: 'I got a lot.'
Jennifer: 'I got more.'
Adam: 'We all got more.'
Suzanne has begun cleaning up, and Elizabeth replaces her at the table: 'Sometimes the glumps get so big they can be shared.'

Eight children are now working at the table. She turns to a child at the easel who calls to her: 'You covered the *whole* space.' To a child at the table: 'It feels sticky. Rub in some flour.'

Jennifer: 'It feels sticky.'

Julie: 'I need some flour!'

Elizabeth: 'Let's leave the flour at that space. Who picked up David's ball? It's nice to have a glump there waiting for a child when he comes.'

Jennifer: 'It's still sticky.'

Sue: 'Can you give me some flour?'

Several children ask for more flour. *Elizabeth* responds: 'It's supposed to stay soft. Yours is just right,' she says, feeling it. 'It's not sticky. If we put too much flour in it, it gets dry and hard, and it isn't fun to use.' Carin has rolled her dough into a ball. Joe has pounded his flat. He begins pressing his finger into his dough. Carin watches and does the same. Sue announces that she is 'all finished.' *Elizabeth* begins to get closure as morning meeting is eminent: 'Andrea, do you need to wash your hands?'

As the transcript above indicates, words frequently accompany actions. And children perform many of the actions. The flour, salt, oil and playdough are all named. The children 'measure' them and put them in a 'bowl'. They also use ingredients to make other things. Just as the teachers use language to describe their actions, so do some of the children. Adam explains that he has to wash his hands, 'I was playing in the sandbox again.' He notes that he is 'spilling flour'. And Andrea concurs, 'I'm spilling it on my dress and on the flour.' As children work the dough, they comment: 'I'm making a dinosaur.' 'I'm making an island.' Language frequently is used to comment on what is happening to things and serves to distinguish a child's activity from that of others.

The children's actions and words become a stimulus for unplanned problem solving: 'What is an island? ... What's it made of ... What's all around an island? ... How do you get there? ... Is it possible to get there on a ship?' The teacher is reluctant to correct a child, reluctant to respond negatively or 'give' an answer. She works and re-works the problem. Her correction is indirect: 'It might be fun to make an island in the sandbox and pour water all around it to make an ocean.' Earlier she simply ignores a child's seeming suggestion that 'light red' is 'Salt!'

Finally, the teachers typically offer positive suggestions. As in the above interchange, it is relatively uncommon for a teacher to correct a child by saying, 'No, it is this.' Yet there is at the same time a good deal of implicit control evident in the indirection and in the frequent occurrences in which a teacher will offer a child a choice of two alternatives the teacher herself already has pre-selected ('Would you like a red one or a blue one?' 'Would you like green paper or pink paper?')

Language to modulate choice

The teachers appear to be uncomfortable with an overtly authoritarian stance. In the above vignette, teachers are shown to frequently use what linguists call 'indirect directives'.

'Would you like to sit in that seat over there?'
'Would you like to put the salt in the bowl?'
'Adam, can you put the oil in?'

Rather than direct a child to act, the teachers appear to expect a child to act. The emphasis is on control whereby the child chooses to conform to adult expectations, because it is the reasonable thing to do ('. . . you'll be closer.' 'If we put too much flour in, it gets dry and hard, and it's not fun to use.')

Such indirection is a common form of speaking with children:

A child cries and several children run from the table where they are working to see what happened. Roxanne, the teacher there, follows them: 'Sally, Brad, would be like to come back and finish your picture?'

A child has been placing pegs in a pegboard. Elizabeth hands the child a margarine cup. 'Would you like to put all the *green* ones in here?' The child picks out an orange peg. 'You want to put the *orange* ones in?' Elizabeth hands him three cups. He fills each in turn with a mixed variety of colors.

Table 3 demonstrates how such examples are only the first level of attempt to influence a child's behavior. 'Would you like' statements appear to characterize situations in which the teacher is not terribly invested. The child does have a choice, and fieldnotes reveal many occasions (as above) in which the child chooses to do otherwise.

Other attempts to influence behavior are increasingly more directive. A second level attempt is slightly more so. 'Let's,' 'please,' or 'I'd like you to . . .' statements convey the notion that something *needs* to be done. The child's cooperation is both invoked and assumed. Third order attempts are considerably more directive: 'It's time for you to do some drawing' — often accompanied by physical action (taking a child by the hand, leading a child to a different area). The child is given little choice in the matter. Finally, but considerably less common, are the fourth-level directives. In the few instances I observed these very direct statements were invoked either because a child, with great effort and deliberation, refused to respond to level 1–3 statements, or, more often, because a child had engaged in some form of aggressive behavior:

> Elizabeth prepares to read a book. 'I'd like you to put your books away. Remember to keep your hands in your laps, while people put their books away.' Elizabeth sends Chris to help Suzanne get snack ready. [He has been causing some commotion.] Erin stands in front of the book, and several children voice complaints. 'It's sitting time, Erin. It isn't snack time.' Erin sits, then stands again. Elizabeth pulls her down without words and continues to read. Erin pops up again. 'Sit down! Sit down! You're disturbing the other children!' By now, Erin has a look of the boldest determination. She rises soon after. 'Sit, Erin!' Elizabeth pulls her legs out in front of her and holds them, reading all the while and directing her attention at the other children.

> Charles grabs Rebecca and throws her on the floor. Roxanne runs to him in horror: 'No, no, no!' She kneels next to him, holding his shoulders. 'Don't you *ever* let me see you do that again. Look at me, Charles. That could hurt!' Roxanne sets Rebecca in her lap. Rebecca sobs gently.

The teacher's degree of involvement was observed to escalate if a child's behavior was seen as detrimental to others.

Though the statements themselves are not dissimilar, fourth-order directives differ from third-level in the degree of non-verbal involve-

Table 3: *Levels of Intensity in Verbal Messages at the Preschool*

Level 4	'Sit down, sit down ...' 'No, no, no!' (accompanied by actions of containment)
Level 3	'It's time for you to ...' (often accompanied by physical action)
Level 2	'Let's ...' 'Please ...' 'I'd like you to ...'
Level 1	'Would you like ...'

ment of the teacher. As in the above examples, the teachers are visibly angry, physically contain (and not merely lead) the children in question, and the statements are themselves delivered with considerably more volume and force. Statements appear to be used differentially, contextually, and largely unconsciously.

Though much of the socialization children seem to experience is implicit, conflict brings rules, values and norms to the fore.

> Four children play together in the house area and around the climbing dome. *Charles* to Tom: 'You can't have my gun!' He walks away, then returns, smiling. 'Bang, bang, bang!' He turns and fetches a block, then comes back again. *Tom* and *Sue* and *Jennifer*: 'Don't get by him. He's a bad guy!' *Sue* goes to the telephone: 'I got to call the police!' Into the receiver: 'Hi, fireman.' *Tom* takes the phone from her. 'Please come here *fast*! Just then, *Elizabeth* comes up to Charles. She turns to me: 'Is he playing G-U-N-S?' She spells the letters out crisply with a look of horror on her face. 'Charles, we don't pretend to have guns in school, even with fingers, because it scares some children. Would you like to do something peaceful with that block? Would you like to build with it?' She leads him to the block area.

In this example, the teacher mixes levels, giving a firm message ('We don't . . .') and appearing to offer a choice to insure compliance. In fact, however, the child is led 'to do something peaceful with that block'.

It was interesting in this instance to see how the rules got internalized (or partly internalized) by the children. Two weeks later the following conversation was transcribed:

> Two boys are playing with bristle blocks behind the house area. One shows the other his 'construction.'
> *Adam:* 'Does it have any guns or powers?'
> *Steve:* 'No, no guns at school.'
> *Adam:* (walking away) 'These aren't guns.'
> Later . . .
> *David:* 'Are these Star Wars ships?'
> *Adam:* 'Yeah!'
> *David:* 'They aren't guns' (shaking his head). The boys begin flying their bristle block ships around the room. Occasionally David contorts his face and makes Darth Vader noises. Chuck joins in.
> *David:* 'That's Hans Solo. This is Luke Skywalker.'
> *Adam:* 'Yeah. I'm Hans Solo.'

> *David:* 'Let's say one of those shot me.'
> *Adam:* 'Yeah, and one shot him the same way.'
> *Elizabeth* comes over to him: 'David, I'm painting everyone's fingernails red. Would you like me to paint *your* fingernails red?'
> *David:* 'No.'
> *Elizabeth:* 'O.K., let me see if Adam would like to come.'
> *David* runs to the climbing dome. He calls to Chuck: 'Come on, let's pretend I'm Luke Skywalker!'

Sometimes a teacher will verbally affirm the action she wants a child to perform, but the affirmation itself is tangential, directed but not directed to the child or children in question.

> A child 'tattles' to the teacher that another child has not put his book away before storytime, as requested. The teacher responds: 'It's all right. I'll take care of it. Stephen will be putting his book back soon. You'll see the pictures better if you sit back.'

> Roxanne hands out 'sit upons,' small cushions that the children literally sit upon for music.
> *Roxanne:* 'Lori, would you like a red one or a blue one?'
> *Lori:* 'I don't want anything!'
> *Elizabeth:* 'Soon she'll do it.'
> *Roxanne* turns to another child: 'You can sit on the turtle or on the giraffe.' [The cushions are covered with animal prints.] Lori sits in the middle of the circle for the entire music period but is effectively ignored.

> The teachers and children sit on the floor before roll is taken.
> *Suzanne* says: 'I wish everybody sat like George. He sits well.'

As exemplified above, the classroom environment is modulated by the teachers through much verbal indirection, affirmation, and controlled choice. It is only the occasional 'deviance' of a child who, failing to conform to these methods of social control, calls the methods themselves into question.

Interactive failure: The 'problem child'

As the examples above indicate, the teachers frequently reward 'good' behavior and choose to ignore 'bad'. They act as though reason, given time, will prevail ('Soon she'll do it.'). The teachers are friendly, giving, and highly motivated. They expect the children to be affectionate and friendly, to tend to task and to respond to their suggestions.

Interaction, it has been assumed, implies the transfer of meaning in two directions. In this context, deviance can be defined as the inability or indifference of a subordinate to conform to the meaning structure of those who hold superordinate status. Quite simply, some children don't do what they are told. Yet in this classroom, as perhaps in many middle- to upper middle-class homes, children are seldom *told*. Rather, behavior seems to be influenced through indirection, reason, suggestion and other forms of implicit control.

The 'deviant' child observed in this classroom was noisy when the teachers wanted quiet. Occasionally he would hit another child. And he appeared to have a quite short attention span, spending much time flitting from area to area, antagonizing a child or children and running off again. Not only did he regularly not tend to task, but he responded inappropriately to the teachers' indirect attempts to modify his behavior. For example, he would giggle or run away when a teacher attempted to influence him verbally.

The teachers could be good to children who responded in kind. But this child repeatedly required a heavier hand, more direct (authoritarian) measures, and the teachers were clearly uncomfortable with the change in role which his behavior precipitated. Suzanne, for example, felt 'guilty' when she felt anger toward a child.

One morning Suzanne explained that Charles had taken cough syrup 'and was wild, hanging from the chandeliers. It has taken one of us all morning to deal with him.' She explained that she had called his mother but that she wasn't home: 'I know why!'

Whenever possible, attempts were made to commend him for appropriate or desirable behavior:

> At morning meeting, before clean up, *Suzanne* interrupts Elizabeth: 'May I say something? Charles put the playdough and pieces away. Thank you, Charles. That was good helping.'

Yet, shortly thereafter, Suzanne had walked over to me, face flushed, fists clenched: 'I'm absolutely livid! There are so *many* inappropriate responses constantly to contend with!' Clearly, though a great deal of emphasis is placed on individualism, group norms exist and the teachers have very firm values, clear ideas about the nature of children and of how they should behave.

Interactions at Harmony: Child to Teacher

As suggested above, interactions between teacher and child frequently are initiated by the child. 'Openers' are often bids for attention:

'Watch me! I can jump through the bars!'

'Look at what I made!'

'I have some pencils like that at my house. I have some magic markers, too, and some crayons.'

These 'requests' for approval typically center on what a child can do or has done or on what he or she possesses. In this way it appears that the children have discerned the values of the adults around them, learned that skill, production and unique response warrant special attention.

Children interact easily with the teachers, calling them by their first names. They show little trepidation or reluctance to initiate conversation and they seem to expect the adults to respond, to listen and to assist them as needed. Though the teacher-child ratio is about 1–8, children, especially girls, appear to interact with the teachers more frequently than with each other. A small, fluid group of boys often build with legos, blocks or bristle blocks or re-enact 'Star Wars' or a television show on the climbing dome and jungle gym. This 'peer' interaction generally takes place without teacher input or interference.

Related to the teachers' reluctance to be perceived as authority figures, is the children's own habit of not acting or reacting in a subordinate manner. To some extent it seems that the children perceive the teachers as people there to serve *them*. Again tangential statements mask the reality of the interaction. Children frequently make declarative rather than interrogative statements. 'I want to paint' (while handing a smock to a teacher) means 'Will you help me put my smock on?' The children do not seem in any way concerned that a teacher will *not* do what is wanted. 'There isn't any paint' is, again, a statement of fact which contains an embedded unexpressed request — 'Would you get some?' Interestingly, such statements are strikingly impersonal. They comment on objects or behaviors that need to be fixed or changed, but do not relegate the child to an inferior status.

Interaction at Irving: Teacher to Child

At the Irving Head Start Center children and adults frequently are involved in different activities. The construction of time and space reflect this separation. Time is set aside each day for the adults to attend to adult responsibilities in an area of the classroom that is separate from that occupied by children. The teachers value close peer interaction and support among themselves, but they also maintain a distinction between themselves and the children.

Whereas the authority of adults is implicit and even de-emphasized at Harmony, adult authority at Irving is underscored in several ways. The children are expected to call the teachers by their last names (Mrs. Barker, Miss Washington). The teacher physically sits above the children during group time or stands above, if the children are seated for a project. Language focuses during group time on social knowledge that can be transmitted verbally from adult to children. Typically and throughout the day adults tell children explicitly what is expected of them. The following discussion will examine: the encouragement of obedience and group membership, the transmission of social knowledge from adults to children, the encouragement of convergent response (a 'generalized' vocabulary), adult directives and interactive failure: the 'problem child.'

The encouragement of obedience and group membership

In the context of an environment where the teachers are responsible for many duties, where they account to and are supervised by others, a great deal of time is spent meeting the demands and erstwhile expectations of authority figures outside the classroom and school. Though the official policy of the metropolitan Head Start governing agency advocates 'play', variety, and individual expression, very different values and beliefs, as mediated through the instructional process, are in evidence in the day-to-day.

Ultimately, the teachers appear to re-create and extend the same authority structure of which they are a part, socializing children into the reality that they themselves experience. They must do what is expected of them and so must the children whom they teach. In particular, the head teacher perceived the notion of 'play' as 'just babysitting', registered concern that children, after a year in her care, 'wouldn't know anything', and repeatedly interpreted situations in which children had 'freedom' or 'choice' as situations that were 'out of control'.

Despite the fact that a different head teacher was in charge of the classroom during the month of September, basic patterns of interaction between adults and children were much the same throughout the year. The first teacher spent large amounts of time in 'teacher space', venturing into the children's area during free play to briefly decrease the noise level or to inhibit certain kinds of play.

'Boys and girls, listen, if I have to tell you not to play so roughly, not to hurt each other, we won't have free play time anymore. We'll all go sit on the red rug and put our heads on our laps.'

'Boys, we don't run with trucks like that.'

'Girls and boys, let's clean up this house like it was when you found it, or you won't be able to play with it anymore.'

(While waiting for children to return from the restrooms) 'If I see you talking, we won't go outside.'

As these examples indicate, the first teacher makes frequent and explicit statements of rules and expects compliance. Her remarks are premised on 'Grandma's Law' ('If you don't, then I won't . . .') She often addresses the children as aggregates ('Boys and girls', 'Boys . . .', 'Girls . . .', 'Girls and boys . . .') And the directives that follow are attempts to make it clear that they will do as she expects or suffer the consequences (though, in fact, consequences seldom followed).

Miss Washington, the aide, reprimands the children in similar fashion, here making an exceptionally explicit statement of 'Grandma's Law':

'This is a game: When we go to the restrooms we have to be quiet. If we're not, it will upset other people. The other part of the game is that, if you don't, you're going to get punished for it. You have to have respect for other people.'

Or, singling out a specific child:

'Kincaid, do you know I'm gonna take your nose home with me. I'm gonna take it home, if you're not quiet.'

Moreover, obedience is often expected *as a group*. The most common breakdown of the total group is not into individuals but rather into groups according to sex. (See examples above.) At Harmony children go to the restrooms willy-nilly as the (individual) need arises, and children use the same facilities. At Irving children queue in different lines according to sex and walk as a group to the respective restrooms. But, throughout the day, children are addressed in aggregates: 'Boys, it's time to clean up', 'Girls, get in line', 'Boys, go get your jackets.'

Most frequently children are singled out as individuals because they have done something 'bad' or inappropriate. Occasionally, a child would shove or hit another; however, the most common occasion for reprimanding is talk when quiet is expected.

'Kincaid, you'll be sorry if I have to come over there.'

'Kerra, don't let me hear another word.'

'Danny, I don't want to have to call your name again.'

At the Center children are regularly expected to be quiet for as much as one and one half hours per morning (during clean-up, the trip to the restrooms, waiting, group time and rest time). Occasionally quiet during breakfast and lunch is also expected.

Children are also singled out when they are not doing what the teacher intends.

'Sanford, don't write on your paper.'

'No, Danny, wait for me.'

Because there is usually only one appropriate response, this too is a relatively frequent occurrence.

The transmission of social knowledge from adults to children

The knowledge the children are expected to know is learned in situations in which the group attends to what the adult says. Throughout the year group instruction revolved around three main activities: recall of birthdate, address, and phone number, recognition of names, and familiarity with the month, date and year. Questions are formed as questions that require one right answer, rather than as problems with multiple solutions. The knowledge valued in the classroom is social in nature: addresses, phone numbers, birthdates, month, day, and week. The nature of the knowledge valued is often such that the children cannot be given information to help them figure it out.

> *Miss Washington:* 'Rob, where do you live? What street do you live on?
> Where does Mr. Kane take you?'
> *Rob:* [no response]
> *Miss Washington:* 'I want you to know that. Dwayne?'
> *Dwayne:* 'Down there.'
> *Miss Washington:* 'Cynthia?'
> *Cynthia:* 'On Condor.'
> *Miss Washington:* 'What number on Condor.'
> *Cynthia:* [can't hear]

This exercise was repeated throughout the year, yet some children still did not know their address, phone number and birthdate at the end of the year.

Perhaps the most distinguishing feature of these exercises is that, when a question is asked, it is frequently asked of every child in the room. Thus, individuation is itself uniform. The underlying value of 'equality' appears to greatly influence the mode of group instruction. One, two, or three questions could take the entire group time. Yet, since the questions were the same and the answers different, the children were not likely to benefit from the repetition.

The encouragement of convergent response

During group instruction, there is an attempt to teach the 'right' answer. The subject matter that defines instruction requires that that children converge on the correct response. Here Mrs. Barker conducts group time:

> *Mrs. Barker:* 'Kincaid, when we're in a group, what are we supposed to do?'
> *Kincaid:* 'Be quiet.'
> *Mrs. Barker:* 'And how are we supposed to sit, Cynthia?'
> *Cynthia:* [can't hear]
> *Mrs. Barker:* 'No, no, no! Sanford?'
> *Sanford:* 'Sit with legs crossed.'
> *Mrs. Barker:* 'Yes, sit like little Indians, with our hands in our laps. What is the name of this month?'
> *Child:* [can't hear]
> *Mrs. Barker:* 'October. Today is Tuesday and yesterday was Monday. Whose birthday was it yesterday?'
> *Child:* 'Beverly's [her first name].'
> *Mrs. Barker:* 'No. Whose birthday was it so we didn't have school?'
> [No response]
> *Mrs. Barker:* 'Columbus' birthday.'
> *Child:* 'She's a girl.'
> *Mrs. Barker:* 'No, Columbus is a man.'

Conformity is expected in terms of quiet, body posture and response. The questions require a 'right' answer. Unlike the preschool, where 'wrong' answers are frequently reworked or ignored (for example, the 'island'), here the teacher is quick to correct a child: 'No, no, no!'

Group consensus is more important than individual expression. For example, in the interaction between Suzanne and the children working with playdough, the teacher grants that 'trees' and 'roads' are 'around islands'. Here Mrs. Barker asks the children to listen to an Ella Jenkins record, 'I'm Changing':

> 'The lady will ask you to sing along, but I don't want you to. I just want you to listen. I worked at another school, and the children really liked the fifth part. They learned this song, and maybe you can, too. I just want you to listen ...'
> [After the record]
> *Mrs. Barker:* 'And we are changing, too.'
> *Child:* 'Like changing the TV channel.'
> *Mrs. Barker:* 'No, not the TV. We're changing our bodies.'
> *Tamara:* 'We're changing our names, too.'
> *Mrs. Barker:* 'No, not our names.'

The children begin to explore the different meanings of changing, but, since the record refers to a specific kind of change, the children's alternative interpretations are considered 'wrong'.

Highly differentiated experience and highly differentiated language seem to be at odds with the basic values of group consensus and solidarily. Words are used less for elaboration and distinction. For example, early in the year most of the children went in the van for a health check-up. Two high school volunteers helped the few children left to cut pictures from magazines.

> *Rob:* 'Where's my stuff?'
> *Vol:* 'Right here.' [She points to his paste.] 'Do you see any food?'
> *Kincaid:* 'No, I see some cake.' [He points to a strawberry chiffon pie and cuts it out.]
> *Vol:* 'Look, there's some food.' [He starts to cut it.] 'And there's some on the the back, too.'
> *Kincaid:* 'There is some more food!'
> Rob rips a picture from the magazine and tears it up.
> *Observer:* 'You didn't like that one?'
> *Rob:* 'I'm trying to find some more food ... I don't like that ... Um-m-m-m yummy food ... Hey, get your thing off of my ... [Kincaid has put his magazine on Rob's paste.] Hey, where's that piece o' pie? I lost that piece o' pie. There's no more food in mine. All the food gone. All my food gone. All my food gone now. Give me my stuff' [reaching for the paste].

Children frequently use generalized terms ('stuff,' 'food,' 'thing') and are not usually encouraged to adopt more specialized or differentiated vocabularies.

There appears to be a striking difference between the use of a generalized term which makes reference to many types of things and an abstraction which is a superordinate classification for more specific objects and events which have been experienced and which can be named. As elaborated in the previous chapter, the Head Start children are encouraged to experience the world as others do, to seek similarity and convergence; a common language or generalized vocabulary reflects this. The preschool children are socialized to a world that is variable, and abstractions order and flux and multiplicity that is fundamental to their experience. They experience 'number' as many things that are available to count, five painted fingers with a number '5', manipulatives that require children to match dots and numbers, etc. Other classificatory systems (for fruit, vegetables, plants, colors, etc.) are similarly differentiated. In short, the more general terms refer to and classify a broad range of objects that the child has encountered over time.

Adult directives

Language is an important means of ensuring conformity. Statements made to children at Irving are generally direct and devoid of options, innuendo, or tangential remarks, affirmative or otherwise.

> 'Boys, get on your yellow line. Now girls . . . Now when you go inside the toilets, no screaming, no wrassling, boys. I'm comin', too.'

> 'Don't go in the house area.'

> 'There's no sleeping together.'

> 'You *must* lay down. You have to. You *must*.'

Most notably, these remarks are consonant with the teachers' beliefs that the children have to do what they are told. There is in language a noticeable absence of what was previously characterized as level one and two remarks, that is, remarks of the 'Would you like', 'Please', or 'I'd like you to . . .' variety. Just as children are restricted temporally and spatially, the intention is clearly to convey to children that they must stay within the limits defined by adults. Their intentional compliance is not being invoked.

Yet meaning is not conveyed through words alone. A great deal of adult meaning is conveyed non-verbally. For this reason it is inadequate to describe teacher-child interaction in terms of words alone. An exercise that in print might appear rigid and drill-like could seem quite different when combined with lilting intonation and gesture. Miss Washington's words occasionally sound severe, even fearsome. Yet her voice is mellow, and her personality conveys warmth and acceptance. In this instance, in the middle of a repetitive exercise, she bursts into laughter and hugs the child, as though they are both trapped in a thoroughly ludicrous predicament.

> *Miss Washington:* 'Your address is 318 Moore Street, and your phone number is 555–2891. Now don't forget it. Laconda?'
> *Laconda:* 'I don't know.'
> *Miss Washington:* [laughing] 'You got to say: "Tell me, tell me, tell me, momma. I *got* to know!"'

And Mrs. Barker could quench anyone's enthusiasm for fidgeting and instill utter silence simply by raising her voice slightly and using sarcasm. The synchrony of style is difficult to render, yet the effect was magical, and it never failed to have the intended result.

In this regard, it is important to note that, though 'Grandma's Law' is a common type of statement, children, in fact are rarely punished. The children do not cringe in fear. In no way are they beaten into submission. Rather such statements are more stimuli than threats. They are intended, and they serve, to terminate a particular form of behavior.

Interactive failure: The 'Problem child'

Interaction in the Irving Head Start Center is characterized by the directness with which children are addressed. It is clear what is expected of them: children are to follow instructions, to listen and to 'work'.

Non-conformity is perceived as 'deviance'. Many actions which in the preschool are considered acceptable are not so in the center. Talking among children is frequently reprimanded, since many of the activities require listening and total group attention. Likewise, 'play' that detracts from the group orientation is discouraged.

The most common infraction of the rules is talking when quiet is expected. One child (Kincaid) was the focus of much teacher disapproval during the fall. The slightest twitch or utterance seemed cause for teacher comment. And yet, Kincaid was round, friendly and endearing. Inevitably, such reprimands were reinforcing, and he would smile broadly. The teachers' attitude toward him was on the order of 'boys will be boys'. His antics were reprimanded frequently but good-naturedly.

When Kincaid left the Center to attend a day care center full-time, another child, Dan, became the focus of attention. While other children's behavior (talking, getting out of line, wrestling, etc.) might be ignored, a day seldom went by in which Dan would not be reprimanded several times. An interesting comparative subanalysis of these children and the child at Harmony would have perhaps informed the larger picture had a more detailed description been attempted in context.

Interaction at Irving: Child to Teacher

Children at Irving have far less interactive time with adults. They tend to play with other children, to 'work' with adults during formalized group times. They are expected to be quiet during these times, except when called on to give a specific response.

During meals, free play, lining up, waiting or resting children frequently do address one of the teachers:

'Miss Washington, Dan pushed me.'

'Mrs. Barker, Keera is talking.'

'Miss Washington, he took my straw.'

These pleas typically are pleas for justice and attempts to bring other children into line in accordance with group norms. As described above, such behavior is also in evidence at the preschool. (See the description of 'Sue' in the discussion of the use of space at Harmony.)

What is noticeably less apparent, however, are remarks that call attention to individual discoveries (the environment changes little), individual products (activities tend to be group projects that look alike), or individual achievements. Because of the general group orientation there is less cause for children to distinguish themselves from the group and such verbalization from the children themselves are far less in evidence. Common experience reinforced day after day appears to encourage children to respond as their peers and to attend to the directives of the teachers.

9   *Summary Analysis*

Anthropologists have sought to understand enormous cross-cultural differences in human behavior within the contexts in which those behaviors occur. Culture and personality anthropologists have examined how cultural characteristics are reproduced and perpetuated within a culture by analyzing the interrelationship among environmental factors broadly conceived, the adaptive response made by adults to those factors, and the mechanisms through which adaptations are conveyed to children. Importantly, the perspective provides insight into the human capacity to construct alternative environments as adaptations to specific circumstances.

Using two early education classrooms as 'windows' through which to observe the child rearing practices of two sets of women, the present study has attempted to delineate how cultural values and attitudes are transmitted to children. In these settings, which are approximately the same size and located in the same community in middle America, the teachers have been shown to construct different orders based on their differing life experiences. At the Irving Head Start Center, teachers and students are black and from working-class backgrounds; at the Harmony preschool, teachers and students are white and middle-class.

Both the black and the white women in the respective settings have clear ideas about how children learn and about how they should behave. They convey their own life orientations and expectations to children by creating total environments that reinforce values that give their own lives meaning. The learning environments thus become different means of reaching different ends. The Head Start teachers work closely together and reinforce collective values; the preschool teachers work alone with children much of the time and encourage values of individualism and self-expression.

The present study has had two major dimensions: first, to compare the child rearing strategies of women in two early education settings and to demonstrate how they differ and, secondly, to explain how these differences arise within different social contexts. In both cases, the teachers live in families very like those of the children they teach, and, in both cases, they structure an environment that is consonant with their experiences outside of school.

Environmental Differences

From slavery to Selma the history of American Blacks has been characterized by prejudice, repression and inequity, and Black Americans, like their African forebears, have adapted to a hostile environment by binding closely with one another. Many writers have noted the importance of 'kin' in the Black community. Black women frequently rear children cooperatively rather than separately.

In the lives of the women discussed here differences in family structure are distinguishing characteristics. The three Harmony teachers live in nuclear families in single family dwellings. All three women are married, are able to share household chores, and take responsibility themselves for specific child rearing tasks.[1] The Head Start teachers, by contrast, both live in extended families, one in a household with her mother (who is bedridden), her father, her own two daughters, her sister, brother-in-law and their daughter, one in a rented house with her son, daughter and granddaughter. Though each makes less than $5,000 per year, they provide major financial support for their families.

Differences in School Environments

The Harmony Preschool

The preschool teachers appear to exercise some degree of control over their work situations; all work part-time by choice in a non-sectarian preschool located within a community church. Within the school setting, the teachers experience some constraints. For example, wall-to-wall carpeting was installed in the room which also seconds as a church meeting room. However, they had a platform made so they could still have paint, water and sand in the classroom. And they have free reign in terms of the curriculum they will provide, the scheduling of activities, and the general organization of the program.

The pastor's office overlooks the A-frame, high-ceilinged room. However, I never observed either he or his secretary enter the room while class was in session, and telephone messages were discreetly dropped into the room on a line. Likewise, parents seemed to hover in the corridor outside and only entered when the children were singing songs or when the teachers otherwise indicated that activities were winding down. The classroom, like the traditional middle-class home, was the domain of women whose main role and function was the care and educating of the young.

The Irving Head Start Center

A powerful bureaucracy structures the administration of local Head Start programs, and personnel at each level are responsible for reporting on the people under them. The supervisor visits unexpectedly or calls to say that she drove by at 7:30 a.m. and did not see the teachers' cars; in turn, she reports her findings. The teachers resent this intrusion, also her imposition of values (such as the advocacy of 'play'), for she is perceived as an 'outsider', someone who never works in the classroom herself. Yet the teachers' job likewise is defined by demands of the system, and they too must go into parents' homes and 'rate' them. Their ambivalent relationship with parents, in part, is created by this extension of the monitoring role.

The bureaucratic structure creates an atmosphere of vigilance and extraneous control that has a kind of 'ripple effect'. This appears to bind the teachers together, uniting them against those who neither understand nor participate in the reality which they share.

However, the teachers are inevitably bound to this greater system even within the classroom. The telephone rings frequently, and it is not uncommon for someone to arrive at the door unexpectedly. Be it a parent, the bus driver, the supervisor, someone from the central office, a member of the ancillary staff, or another teacher in the building, one teacher or the other must interrupt what she is doing. Differences in 'lag' time (See Figure B) are indicative of the fact that the Head Start teachers are subjected to more external disruption.

Not only do the Head Start teachers experience less personal control over their situations than the preschool teachers, they also have more extensive responsibilities both at work and at home. Ironically, the social service demands of the program appear to create a situation not unlike that which Black women have been shown to experience in the society at large (Stack, 1975).

Adaptations

In both settings, the teachers' beliefs and behaviors appear to be influenced by and continuous with their experience outside of school. Whereas the preschool teachers re-create a setting quite like that found within nuclear families, one in which women spend a great deal of time in child-centered interactions, the Head Start teachers appear to re-enact patterns of interaction that have been shown to prevail within extended family networks (Hill, 1972; Stack, 1975; and Nobles, 1974), working closely together, sharing tasks, decisions, and resources, and sharing also the perception of those outside as hostile to their interests and efforts.

The preschool women work alone with children much of the morning, encouraging children also to work alone, making 'unique' products and fostering language that will enable the individual child to differentiate his/her experience from that of others. The Head Start women work together most of the morning, and, in their structuring of events, provide group-oriented activities that encourage children to do what others do.

Adaptations Conveyed through Interactions with Children

The structuring of time and space, the choice of activities and utilization of materials and patterns of adult-child interaction have been shown to be implicit forms through which adult values are transmitted to children. The two programs have been shown to differ systematically. It is as though the dynamic in the preschool was a sort of centrifugal force, working children away from the group, while the Head Start center dynamic was centripetal, encouraging children to cohere and to be part of the group. In their focus on individual children and in their structuring of an environment that maximizes individual choice and action, the preschool teachers encourage children to be uniquely different from others. 'Free time' provides time for children to select activities of interest. Time is a continuum through which both children and activities change. Because children 'develop' (or change) over time the teachers provide different materials for children of different ages and separate the children into three different age groups for 'developmentally appropriate' activities.

For much of the morning individuals move in different directions, at different rates of speed. Likewise time can be broken out into 'units'. And the classroom space is highly-differentiated, providing different activities in different areas of the room. Transformational materials

Table 4:   *Systematic differences between settings*

	Preschool	Head Start Center
Time		
How spent	Individual 'alone'	Group — doing what others do
How structured	Continuum-changing	Container- -repetitive
How focused	Child-centered	Peer-centered
Space		
How structured (form)	Shared by adults and children	Separate spaces for adults and children
How used (function)	Free flow of movement (individuals moving in different directions at different rates of speed)	Clustered into group activities
Activities and Materials		
How structured	Linear	Repetitive
For what purpose	Individuation multiplicity differentiation	Group Consensus social bonding establishment of adult authority
	Orientation to change	Orientation to the repeated act
Expected responses	Divergent; object-oriented	Convergent; person-oriented
Materials	Transformational Highly organized (differentiated)	Unchanging
Patterns of Interaction	The encouragement of individuality	The encouragement of obedience and group membership
	Teaching through explication and differentiation of experience (the development of a 'particularized' vocabulary)	The transmission of social knowledge from adults to children and the encouragement of convergent response (a 'generalized' vocabulary)
	The modulation of choice	Adult directives

provide opportunities for children to have unique experiences, to make unique products, to impose their own order onto things. Teachers spend most of their time in the classroom with the children, and they are generally responsive to their requests. Children frequently initiate conversations with the teachers, and they call them by their first names. The classroom thus would seem to reinforce values of individuality and autonomy and to promote positive feelings toward change.

The Head Start teachers appear to structure time, space and activity so as to reinforce values of collectivism, authority and traditional (repetitive) modes of interaction that reinforce the group experience. Children spend most of their time together in group activities, and social knowledge conveyed through verbal exchange appears more important than the manipulation of things.

But the adults likewise spend much of their time together, engaged in a proliferation of tasks that are integral to the social service demands of the program. A separate 'teacher space' is set up to provide a place for these duties to be accomplished. The 'peer-centered' nature of the classroom is evident not only in the bond between the women who share tasks and problems, but also in the 'smoke-screen' maintained by the peer group that gives the illusion of conforming to authority.

By structuring time, space and activity so that children do what others do, while also conforming to the directives of the teachers, the teachers thus seem to socialize children to adapt to the reality which they themselves experience.

Toward a Theory of Cultural Transmission

Though understanding how children become group members and how group norms are reproduced and perpetuated in schools is a timely concern, a theory of education as cultural transmission has yet to be developed (Wilcox, 1982b). Based on observation of the enculturation processes in two classrooms in middle America, the following models isolate constellations of factors that help to explain how adaptations to specific environments are transmitted to children.

A theoretical model is a specific form of a theory, highlighting key relationships between factors which are thought to be significant. In these cases, the models isolate factors that appear to be adaptive responses to differing environments and postulate how these alternative adult orientations might have subsequent outcomes in the behavioral and cognitive styles of children. Extending anthropologists' belief that a culture is a self-perpetuating system (Cohen, 1971), the models provide a framework for understanding how child rearing practices, as express-ed in different environments, may serve to perpetuate social and cognitive characteristics within a population.

Adult-Individualistic

Importance of experimentation; knowledge gained from the manipulation of things

Piaget proposes that children gradually learn to abstract from their experience in the concrete world by acting on objects during the early

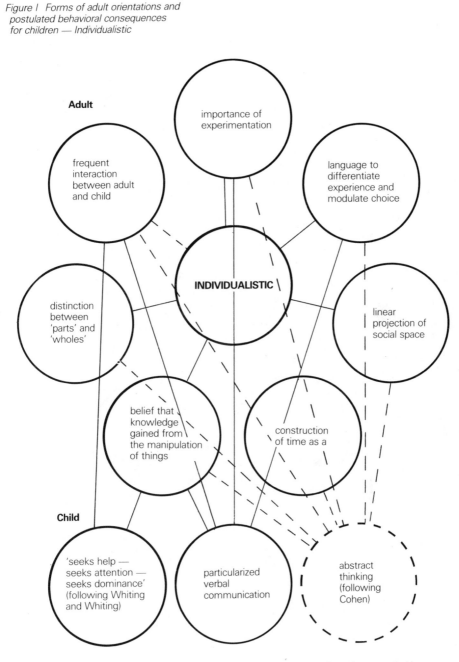

Figure I Forms of adult orientations and postulated behavioral consequences for children — Individualistic

connections demonstrated in present study

hypothesized connections

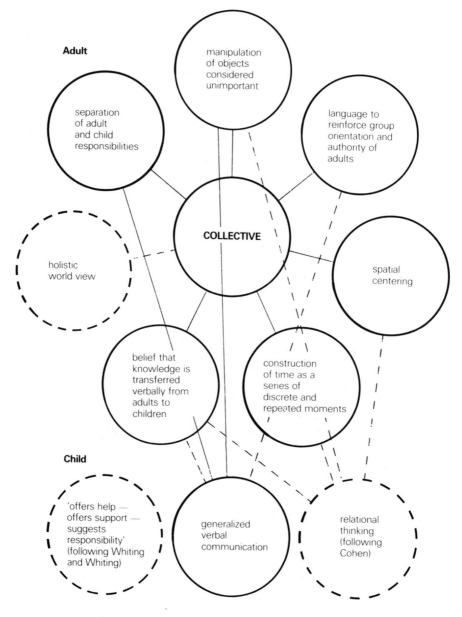

Figure J Forms of adult orientations and
postulated behavioral consequences
for children — Collective

Adult

manipulation
of objects
considered
unimportant

separation
of adult
and child
responsibilities

language to
reinforce group
orientation and
authority of
adults

COLLECTIVE

holistic
world view

spatial
centering

belief that
knowledge is
transferred
verbally from
adults to
children

construction
of time as a
series of
discrete and
repeated moments

Child

'offers help —
offers support —
suggests
responsibility'
(following Whiting
and Whiting)

generalized
verbal
communication

relational
thinking
(following
Cohen)

connections demonstrated in
present study
hypothesized connections

years of life. He called the young child a 'little scientist', who constantly strives to understand the natural world. In the preschool the teachers assume that 'acting on objects' is important. They provide materials that can be transformed into many things, and, through experimentation, children 'discover' possibilities inherent in those materials. In a seemingly significant way, teachers assume that, once children have *experienced* something, they will *know* it. ('It might be fun to make an island in the sandbox and pour water all around it to make an ocean.')

Language to differentiate experience and modulate choice

The emphasis on the individual child, the changing nature of the curriculum, and the transformational nature of materials provide opportunities for increasingly differentiated experience. As Bernstein (1971) hypothesizes: 'the greater the differentiation of the child's experience, the greater his ability to differentiate and elaborate objects in his environment' (p. 28). Children are encouraged to enumerate characteristics of an object. A pineapple is 'brown' and 'round', 'sweet' and 'prickly'. Levels of intensity in the verbal directives of adults require children to decode what is being allowed and/or encouraged.

Distinction between 'parts' and 'wholes'

The room is divided into different areas, and children are allowed to move from section to section; the curriculum is divided into 'units' and even the group is a whole composed of parts ('Who is missing?'), composed of children who are frequently called by name and whose names appear on boards on the wall. The nature of the curriculum is such that superordinate classifications (fruit, number, etc.) are constantly being broken down into their component parts.

Linear projection of social space

Children spend much of the morning moving in different directions at different rates of speed.

Construction of time as a continuum

The teachers believe that children 'develop' in different ways and at different rates of speed. By providing an environment that offers choices, by working closely with the children, and by implementing a curriculum that changes over time, they strive to facilitate the 'growth' of the individual child.

Interaction between adults and children

The preschool teachers are able to work with the children most of the morning. They sit with groups of children in specific areas of the room for much of the morning 'free play' time. They help children clean up, sit .with their age-groups of children at snack, lead three ropes of children to the park. For most of the morning time, space and activity are constructed so as to maximize adult-child interaction.

Child-Individualistic

'Seeks help — seeks attention — seeks dominance'

The preschool children generally are able to maximize their interactions with the teachers, gaining access to their attempts to individualize and also gaining attention for their individual efforts. Fieldnotes indicate that more interactions take place between children and teachers than between the children themselves. A group of older boys who frequently generated their own pretend play were the exception.

Verbal communication

Space is usually shared with adults, and conversation is encouraged. Frequently, verbal exchange is related to what the child has done to materials.

Abstract thinking

Cohen (1969/76) presents the argument that abstract thought has three major components: breadth of knowledge, analytic abstraction, and the ability to extract information from an embedding context. Although it was not possible to 'get inside' children's heads, their observable behavior could be seen to lay the groundwork for such an orientation: in their diversity of experience and use of a differentiating vocabulary, in the multiple opportunities they had for experiencing concrete components of classifications (number, fruit, color, etc.) and in the opportunities provided in which they could 'pull out' of a material an aspect they wished to elaborate. Though such experiences seem only tangentially related to the requirements of public schooling, the teachers firmly believed that these experiences were what were appropriate for young children. Interestingly, when I returned to the classroom late in the year, the head teacher greeted me with pride: 'Oh, I'm so glad you've come to see us. We're so proud of our children. Three of them are reading already.'

Adult-Collective

Manipulation of objects unimportant; knowledge transferred from adults to children

The Irving Head Start teachers believe that children learn by listening and by repeating after the teacher. Blocks and other manipulatives are considered playthings, things to keep the children occupied during 'free time', while the teachers attend to other responsibilities. Activities frequently require children to follow directions, to perform the same actions and to arrive at the same product. To this extent, the objects serve as media through which the adults' goals can be realized, rather than as objects of interest in themselves. The focus appears to be on people, not to things.

Language to reinforce the group orientation and authority of adults

The adults in the center share decisions, resources and responsibilities. In interaction with children, it is common for the teachers to give verbal directives to the group, often to aggregates to children ('Boys', 'Boys and girls', 'Girls ..') These directions tend to be quite specific, stipulating a particular place or way in which children are to wait or stand, or a particular way in which a task is to be accomplished (gluing feathers on a band, coloring, etc.) During group time the teacher will often ask the same question of every child in the group, seemingly stressing the equality of group members. Teachers sit or stand above the children. Since they are called by their last names, the authority of adults would likewise seem to be reinforced.

Holistic world view

Although the present study has not addressed this topic directly, a holistic world view would seem to be indicated in the construction of time as a 'container', in the spatial centering of the group for much of each day, in the convergent responses expected from the children, as well as in the aggregating of groups of children according to sex.

Spatial centering

Children spend most of their time at the center 'grouped'. Most ride to school in the same van. They eat breakfast together, wait on the red rug until all are finished. During 'free play' three to four children are assigned to each area and are to remain there. After clean-up, the children have a formal 'group' time: they rest together, and then eat lunch together. In almost every time frame the group is 'centered' on a specific activity.

Construction of time as a series of discrete moments

Time appeared to be constructed as a series of 'containers', in which the same activity was repeated day after day. Time was also divided between adult responsibilities and time for the children.

Separation of adult responsibilities and children

Because the teachers are responsible for many tasks besides purely educational ones, time and space are provided so they can attend to 'adult' responsibilites (providing meals, cleaning up, filling the re-frigerator, ordering supplies, doing paperwork, keeping records, speak-ing with supervisors and ancillary personnel, preparing materials, etc.) In 'teacher space' many of these 'adult' tasks are carried out. In 'children' space, the teachers see to it that the children have breakfast and a rest time, and they interact with the group in formal question-and-answer type lessons that are repeated each day over time.

Child-Collective

'Offers help — offers support — suggests responsibly'

The first day that I entered the Center I was struck by the realization that older children were supervising younger ones while mothers filled out forms and spoke with the teacher and social worker. Although Whiting and Whiting (1975) cite this as a primary personality characteristic of children in kin-based traditional societies, such behavior was not much in evidence in the day-to-day observations of the present study. To some extent, an educational setting with children of the same age places constraints on such behavior, since children more typically 'care' for those younger than themselves.

Generalized verbal communication

At the Center children are with their peers more than with adults. Children frequently use generalized terms such as 'thing' and 'stuff' and are not encouraged through interaction with adults (and through changing and highly differentiated objects) to use more particularized vocabularies. In adult-child interactions the focus on convergence, similarity and agreement appears to be at odds with values of divergence, differentiation and distinction implied by a particularized language.

Relational thinking

Cohen (1969–76) argues that relational thinking is characteristic of persons reared in 'shared function' environments, in family and friendship groups in which functions such as child care, leadership and control of funds are shared rather than being assigned to status roles. Such experiences, she argues, lead to a particular form of conceptual patterning. The relational style 'requires a descriptive mode of abstraction and is self-centered in its orientation to reality; only the global characteristics of a stimulus have meaning to its users, and these only in reference to some total context' (p. 301). She notes that, in addition to incompatible selection and classification rule sets, three other characteristics distinguish relationship thinkers from abstract thinkers: the perception of time as a series of discrete moments, of self in the center of social space, and in specific causality rather than multiple causality. Such conceptual patterning would seem reflective of the patterns of social organization observed in the center.

Conclusion

To suggest a way of looking is an appropriate research enterprise, but to suggest a way of doing things differently is to venture upon the thin ice of social policy. Evidence from the present study lends support to the contention that poor Black children in America do not 'lack stimulation', as the formulators of so many social programs have assumed. Rather they appear to be methodically socialized into the pre-eminent values of a society in which the needs of the group prevail over the needs of the individual. To the extent that values and attitudes are culturally-mediated, to that extent poor Black children can be said to be 'different' from children from white, middle-income families, though, of course, such a generalization would not hold in every instance.

Clearly the collective orientation of Afro-Americans has both historical roots and contemporary efficacy. The Head Start women operate under real constraints both distal and proximal. Yet to lodge the 'problem' in institutional structures is also too simple. For in their ability to work cooperatively, to share resources and responsibilities, to see humor in adversity and to accomplish many tasks which include the care of children, the Head Start women achieve something increasingly beyond the grasp of upwardly mobile America — a oneness with others and a common purpose. Far from being helpless pawns in a system, they actively construct a meaningful and consistent order that 'works' within — and even in opposition to — the constraints of the bureaucratic order and the society at large.

Instead of prescriptions I am left only with parting images:

of Miss Washington's wedding late in the school year as the rhythmic and rising cadences of the soloist exploded in affirmation from the congregation — a song of and for all,

of the reception that followed in which the elderly were both present and participating,

and later, of her mother's funeral, when I saw a retarded woman serving as usher be the first to rush to comfort an anguished family member.

And of images, too numerous to mention, of a broader society which achieves but which also fractures and excludes.

Ultimately it must be realized that differences among peoples within American society are deeply grounded in a social system that is premised on an unequal distribution of resources, a society that is product, more than people, oriented, one in which verbal facility, abstraction and self-achievement are prized to the exclusion of other values.

If policy is to be effected, a first step may be to acknowledge that individuals are not 'right' or 'wrong', that people are not 'culturally deprived', and that social groups do not stretch out along a line from 'primitive' to 'advanced'. Rather we live in a world of multiple orders and multiple meanings, and, if we are to fulfill our most basic needs, both to achieve — and to belong, to change — and to maintain, to grow both individually and together, we must find ways to learn from each other about these seemingly contrary forces. In the social sciences we stand, like Newton, on a beach of sand, looking first at this pebble or this shell, while a sea of truth lay undiscovered before us.

Notes

1 I do not mean to suggest that the preschool teachers had lives that were easy and problem-free. Elizabeth had three children, the youngest an adopted Korean refugee. This child had learning problems that were of great concern to her. Roxanne had only one child, a preschool child in the class, but, because of his age, he required a good deal of attention once they returned home. It is not the intention of this book to compare the teachers in terms of value-laden dichotomies (good/bad, bad/good, easy/hard, etc.). Rather I have attempted to point up constellations of factors that seem to arise within different social contexts.

Epilogue

Classrooms are not isolated from the communities they serve. By studying two classrooms that are continuous with family life, one sees ways in which classrooms connect with the ebb and flow of life outside schools. Similarly, as a researcher wishing to study schools and classrooms, I found my vision blurred, my 'social science' distorted, by my own connections to a particular way of life and to my own biases about what constituted education. The great gift of ethnography is that it humbles us, and, once humbled, we are in a position to learn something.

I have struggled with that learning and still feel unease at my own misunderstanding. Is it fair — or in some way *true* — to characterize the nature of materials in the Head Start center as 'static'? Is there a dynamism there that I have not experienced and thus cannot realize? Or is the word pejorative, insinuating that something is missing when in fact materials and their nature are of little — or less — consequence. Patterns of interaction are dynamic processes; we are not east in stone.

Even now I see only glimpses that give me pause. I know that I would 'naturally' praise an individual child's work, and I was always caught by surprise as four or five other children immediately would look up and wave their papers at me and call for recognition. Praise, like punishment, was frequently distributed to the group as a whole, and my ways were aberrant and strange and probably divisive.

'Group time' was another arena of difference, for Mrs Barker had an air of authority and even majesty that mere words fail to render. When she sat on a chair above the children for group time, wiggling ceased and an instantaneous hush fell over the group. An infraction could be dispelled with the raise of an eyebrow. When I sat down with the group, my non-verbal signals seemingly were less developed, for the children immediately broke into broad grins and began scooting forward! Boys in the back would sometimes start poking one another or giggling. My 'non-directive directives' maintained only an uneasy order or had little effect. Finally one day I yelled at the children, and Mrs Barker applauded from the teachers' area: 'That's it! That's what you have to do! No one can do it for you!'

Research on schools has been dedicated to understanding educational processes by isolating variables, by effecting treatments, by finding some treatments to effect statistically significant change. Once researchers 'know' something, then others are told what to 'do'. It is little wonder so little changes in this world.

In the classroom we were mutually constructing, change, subtle and spontaneous, was occurring as all of us took in new ways of doing things, altered our constructions and tried them on for size. One day I had brought a library book in to read to the children — *The King Who Could Not Sleep.* The children liked it so well they began to ask for it every day. Then one day Mrs Barker came up to me and whispered: 'You have to come see this. You won't believe it . . .' We walked to where we could see Danny sitting on a chair near the pillar. Danny, the class 'problem child', was sitting quietly, utterly absorbed in *The King Who Could Not Sleep.* Mrs Barker was deeply moved: 'I never thought I'd see the day.' Several days later she had Danny on her lap, looking at the book, but in exaggerated words and intonations that emulated and mocked my style. I never even came close to group time majesty.

At base trying to change the world — or anything in it — is trying to make reality conform to the way it makes sense to us, to the way we think things *ought* to be. Early in the year, once I had begun taking on my share of responsibility in the room, Beverly (Mrs Barker) asked Candi and me what we thought we might do for Christmas. I had offered numerous suggestions and was encouraged by her 'Show us'. I made green and red playdough with the children (which, when mixed together, turned artillery grey), brought in catalogues that could be cut up to make 'Wish Books'. We set up paint easels, made cookies, and had several centers going at once. The supervisor arrived one day and was full of praise. Afterwards the head teacher came up to me and said: 'We're going to do *this* from now on!' However, the noise level was at a high pitch, and each day the classroom looked like a disaster area with playdough stuck to the floor and paper scattered in a broad area. The increase in sheer turmoil was more than evident. Within a few weeks the classroom returned to normal.

I didn't understand then, as I was to come to realize later, the havoc such changes wreak in lives already stressed by too little time, too little money, and too much responsibility. Researchers, even participant-observers, often are concerned that their presence will affect what they observe, yet the world does not change so easily, either at our appearance or in response to our intentions. And yet, after a year in this classroom, we walked away with new options and with new understandings.

Such encounters seem small indeed when compared to the great edifice of social science research institutions, merely human when compared to computer printouts that synthesize complex bits of information, so that someday we might understand something, and someday, when enough is known, *do* something.

'Knowing' and 'doing' stand apart. Yet what would happen if, throughout the country, 'knowers' learned to 'do' and 'doers' learned to 'know'? What would happen if teachers themselves had the opportunity to work in different social contexts and the skills — and the luxury — to analyze their own practice? What would happen if teachers from different cultures and races and classes had the opportunity to teach together and to learn from one another? What would happen if, as Lindblom and Cohen (1979) suggest, interaction itself began to be a force for change?

Our science is cast in patterns of propriety, and all our wonderings and longings, our guilt and our frustrations must precede and follow what we do.

Bibliography

ANYON, J. (1980) 'Social class and the hidden curriculum', *Journal of Education*, 162, 1, winter.

ARON, R. (1967) *Main Currents of Sociological Thought*, Vol. 2, New York, Basic Books.

BARATZ, S. and BARATZ, J. (1970) 'Early childhood intervention: the social science base of institutional racism', *Harvard Educational Review*, 40, 1, pp. 29–50.

BECKER, H. (1971) 'Social class variations in the teacher-pupil relationship' in COSIN, B. *et al.* (Eds.) *School and Society: A Sociological Reader*, London, Routledge and Kegan Paul.

BENEDICT, R. (1934) *Patterns of Culture*, Boston and New York, Houghton Mifflin Co.

BERNSTEIN, B. (1971) *Class, Codes and Control*, Vol. 1, London, Routledge and Kegan Paul.

BIRDWHISTELL, R. (1952) *Introduction to Kinesics*, Louisville, University of Louisville.

BIRDWHISTELL, R. (1967) 'Communication as a multi-channel system' in SILLS, D. (Ed.) *International Encyclopedia of the School Sciences*, New York, Crowell-Collier and Macmillan, pp. 24–9.

BLOOM, B. (1964) *Stability and Change in Human Characteristics*, New York, John Wiley and Sons.

BLUMER, H. (1969) *Symbolic Interactionism: Perspective and Method*, Englewood Cliffs, NJ, Prentice-Hall.

BOGDAN, R. and BIKLEN, S. (1982) *Qualitative Research for Education: An Introduction to Theory and Methods*, New York, Allyn and Bacon.

BOWLES, S. and GINTIS, H. (1976) *Schooling in Capitalist America: Educational Reform and the Contradictions of Economic Life*, New York, Basic Books.

BRAINERD, C. (1978) *Piaget's Theory of Intelligence*, Englewood Cliffs, NJ, Prentice-Hall.

BRONFENBRENNER, U. (1958) 'Socialization and social class through time and space' in MACCOBY, E. *et al.* (Eds.) *Readings in Social Psychology*, New York, Henry Holt.

BRONFENBRENNER, U. (1974) A report on longitudinal evaluations of pre-school programs, Vol. 2, *Is Early Intervention Effective?*, DHEW pub no (OHD) 74–25, Washington, DC, Office of Child Development.

BRONFENBRENNER, U. (1976) 'The experimental ecology of education', AERA award address. Paper presented at the annual meeting of the American Educational Research Association, San Francisco, April.

BROPHY, J. (1970) 'Mothers as teachers of their own pre-school children: the influence of socio-economic status and task structure on teaching specifically', *Child Development*, 41, 1, pp. 79–94.

BRUNER, J. (1978) 'The role of dialogue in language acquisition' in SINCLAIR, A., JARVELLA, R. and LEVELT, W. (Eds.) *The Child's Conception of Language*, Berlin/Heidelberg, Springer-Verlag, pp. 241–56.

BRUNER, J, OLIVER, R. and GREENFIELD, P. (1966) *Studies in Cognitive Growth*, New York, John Wiley and Sons.

BUCK-MORSS, S. (1975) 'Socio-economic bias in Piaget's theory and its implications for cross-cultural studies', *Human Development*, 18, pp. 35–49.

BURNETT, J. (1969) 'Culture of the school: a construct for research and explanation in education'. Paper presented at annual meeting of the American Education Research Association, Minneapolis, April.

BURTON, J. and JONES, L. (1982) 'Recent trends in achievement levels of black and white youth', *Educational Researcher*, 11, 4, April, pp. 10–14.

BYERS, P. and BYERS, H. (1972) 'Non-verbal communication and the education of children' in CAZDEN, C. JOHN, V. and HYMES, D. (Eds.) *Functions of Language in the Classroom*, New York, Teachers College Press.

CALDWELL, B. (1967) 'What is the optimal learning environment for the young child?', *American Journal of Orthopsychiatry*, 37.

CAMPBELL, D. and STANLEY, J. (1963) 'Experimental and quasi-experimental designs for research on teaching' in GAGE, N. (Ed.) *Handbook of Research on Teaching*, Chicago, Rand McNally.

CARINI, unpublished workshop notes.

CARNOY, M. and LEVIN, H. (1976) *The Limits of Educational Reform*, New York, Longman Inc.

CHOMSKY, N. (1968) *Language and Mind*, New York, Harcourt, Brace and World.

CICIERELLI, V. (1969) 'Project Head Start, a national evaluation: summary of the study' in HAYS, D. (Ed.) *Britannica Review of American Education*, Vol. I, Chicago, Encyclopedia Britannica.

COHEN, R. (1969) 'Conceptual styles, culture conflict and non-verbal tests of intelligence', *American Anthropologist*, 71, 5, October and in ROBERTS, J. and AKINSANYA, S. (Eds.) (1976) *Schooling in the Cultural Context: Anthropological Studies of Education*, New York, David McKay.

COHEN, Y. (1971) 'The shaping of men's minds: adaptations to imperatives of culture' in WAX, M., DIAMOND, S. and GEARING, F. (Eds.) *Anthropological Perspectives on Education*, New York, Basic Books, pp. 19–49.

COLE, M. and GAY, J. (1976) 'Culture and memory' in ROBERTS, J. and AKINSANYA, S. (Eds.) *Schooling in the Cultural Context: Anthropological*

Studies of Education, New York, David McKay, pp. 322–40.

COLE, M., GAY, J., GLICK, J. and SHARP, D. (1971) *The Cultural Context of Learning and Thinking*, New York, Basic Books.

COLEMAN, J. *et al.* (1966) *Equality of Educational Opportunity*, Washington, DC, US Government Printing Office.

CONDON, W. and SANDER, L. (1974) 'Neonate movement is synchronized with adult speech: interactional participation and language acquisition', *Science*, 183, 4120, 11 January.

COOK, T. and CAMPBELL, D. (1979) *Quasi Experimentation: Design and Analysis Issues for Field Settings*, Chicago, Rand McNally.

CORWIN, R. (Ed.) (1981) *Research in Sociology of Education and Socialization*, Vol. 2, Greenwich, Conn, Jai Press.

DASEN, P. (1972) 'Cross-cultural Piagetian research: a summary', *Journal of Cross Cultural Psychology*, 3, pp. 23–39.

DATTA, L. (1979) 'Another spring and other hopes: some findings from national evaluations of Project Head Start' in ZIGLER, E. and VALENTINE, J. (Eds.) *Project Head Start: A Legacy of the War on Poverty*, New York, Free Press, pp. 405–32.

DECKER, S. (1969) *An Empty Spoon*, New York, Harper and Row.

DE LONE, R. (1978) *Small Futures: Inequality, Children, and the Failure of Liberal Reform*, New York, Harcourt, Brace Jovanovich.

DENNIS, W. (1940) *The Hopi Child*, New York, Appleton-Century.

DEVOS, G. and HIPPLER, A. (1969) 'Cultural psychology: comparative studies of human behavior' in LINDSEY, G. and ARONSON, E. (Eds.) *The Handbook of Social Psychology*, Vol. 3, Reading, Mass, Addison-Wesley Publishing Co, pp. 323–416.

DIAMOND, S. (1971) 'Epilogue', in WAX, M., DIAMOND, S. and GEARING, F. (Eds.) *Anthropological Perspectives on Education*, New York, Basic Books, pp. 300–6.

DOBBERT, M. (1982) *Ethnographic Research: Theory and Application for Modern Schools and Societies*, New York, Praeger.

DOLGIN, J., KEMNITZER, D. and SCHNEIDER, D. (Eds.) (1977) 'As people express their lives, so they are . . .', *Symbolic Anthropology: A Reader in the Study of Symbols and Meaning*, New York, Columbia University Press.

DuBOIS, C. (1944) *The People of Alor*, Minneapolis, University of Minnesota Press.

DUMONT, R. and WAX, M. (1969) 'Cherokee school society and the intercultural classroom', *Human Organization*, 28, 3, pp. 217–26.

DURKHEIM, E. (1933) *On the Division of Labor in Society* (trans by G. Simpson), New York, Macmillan Co.

DURKHEM, E. (1956) *Education and Sociology*, Glencoe, Ill, Free Press.

EDDY, E. (1967) *Walk the White Line: A Profile of Urban Education*, Garden City, NY, Anchor Books.

EDSON, L. (1969) 'Jensenism, n. The theory that IQ is largely determined by the genes', *New York Times Magazine*, 31 August.

EGGAN, D. (1956) 'Instruction and affect in Hopi cultural continuity', *Journal of Anthropological Research*, 12, 4, and in ROBERTS, J. and AKINSANYA, S. (Eds.) (1976) *Schooling in the Cultural Context: Anthropological Studies of Education*, New York, David McKay, pp. 140–56.

ERIKSON, E. (1950) *Childhood and Society*, New York, W W Norton.

ERIKSON, F. (1973) 'What makes school ethnography 'ethnographic'?', *Council on Anthropology and Education Newsletter*, 2, pp. 10–19.

ERICKSON, F. (1979) 'Mere ethnography: some problems in its use in educational practice', *Anthropology and Education Quarterly*, 10, 3, Fall, pp. 182–7.

ERICKSON, F., FLORIO, S. and BREME, D. (1975) 'Children's socio-linguistic performance and teachers' judgment of children's competence', paper presented at the annual meeting of the American Educational Research Association, Washington, DC, April.

ERICKSON, F. and MOHATT, G. (1982) 'Cultural organization of participation structures in two classrooms of Indian students' in SPINDLER, G. (Ed.) *Doing the Ethnography of Schooling: Educational Anthropology in Action*, New York, Holt, Rinehart and Winston, pp. 132–74.

EVERHART, R. (1983) *Reading, Writing and Resistance*, Boston, Routledge and Kegan Paul.

FLAVELL, J. (1963) *The Developmental Psychology of Jean Piaget*, New York, Van Nostrand.

FLORIO, S. and WALSH, M. (1976) 'The teacher as colleague in classroom research', paper presented at the annual meeting of the American Educational Research Association, San Francisco, April.

FORMAN, G. and Kuschner (1977) *The Child's Construction of Knowledge*, Monterey, Calif, Brooks/Cole Publishing Co.

FOX, R. (1967) *Kinship and Marriage*, Harmondsworth, Middx, Penguin Books Inc.

FRAKE, C. (1973) 'The diagnosis of disease among the Subanum of Mindanao', in KEDDIE, N. (Ed.) *Tinker, Tailor; The Myth of Cultural Deprivation*, Harmondsworth, Middx, Penguin Education, pp. 121–48.

FREUD, S. (1920/53) *A General Introduction to Psychoanalysis*, Garden City, NY, Permabooks.

FUCHS, E. (1969) *Teachers Talk: Views from Inside City Schools*, Garden City, NY, Anchor Books.

GAGNÉ, R. (1968) 'Contributions of learning to human development', *Psychology Review*, 75, 3, May, pp. 177–91.

GAY, J. and COLE, N. (1967) *The New Mathematics in an Old Culture: A Study of Learning Among the Kpelle of Liberia*, New York, Holt, Rinehart and Winston.

GEERTZ, C. (1973) *The Interpretation of Cultures*, New York, Basic Books.

GEERTZ, C. (1977) 'From the native's point of view: on the nature of anthropological understanding' in DOLGIN, J., KEMNITZER, D. and

SCHNEIDER, D. (Eds.) *Symbolic Anthropology: A Reader in the Study of Symbols and Meanings*, New York, Columbia University Press, pp. 480–92.

GINSBURG, H. (1972) *The Myth of the Deprived Child: Poor Children's Intellect and Education*, Englewood Cliffs, NJ, Prentice-Hall.

GLADWIN, T. (1970) *East is a Big Bird: Navigation and Logic on Puluwat Atoll*, Cambridge, Mass, Harvard University Press.

GLICK, J. (1975) 'Cognitive development in cross-cultural perspective' in HOROWITZ, F. (Ed.) *Review of Child Development Research*, Vol. 4, Chicago, University of Chicago Press, pp. 595–654.

GORDON, I. (1975) *The Infant Experience*, Columbus, CHARLES E Merrill Publishing Co.

GORDON, I. (1977) 'Parent educaion and parent involvement: retrospect and prospect', paper presented at the 'Toward the Competent Parent' conference at Georgia State University, Atlanta, February.

GRAY, S. and KLAUS, R. (1965) 'An experimental pre-school program for culturally deprived children', *Child Development*, 36, 4, pp. 887–98.

GRAY, S. and KLAUS, R. (1970) 'The early training project: a seventh-year report', *Child Development*, 41, pp. 909–24.

GREENFIELD, P. and BRUNER, J. (1969) 'Culture and cognitive growth' in GOSLIN, D. (Ed.) *Handbook of Socialization Research*, New York, Rand McNally, pp. 633–57.

GUTMAN, H. (1976) *The Black Family in Slavery and Freedom*, New York, Pantheon Books.

HALE, J. (1982) *Black Children: Their Roots, Culture, and Learning Styles*, Provo, Utah, Brigham Young University Press.

HALL, E. (1959) *The Silent Language*, New York, Doubleday.

HALL, E. (1966) *The Hidden Dimension*, New York, Doubleday.

HALL, E. (1977) *Beyond Culture*, Garden City, NY, Anchor Books.

HALLOWELL, A. (1953) 'Culture, personality, and society' in KROEBER, A. *et al*. *Anthropology Today: An Encyclopedic Inventory*, Chicago, University of Chicago Press.

HALLOWELL, A. (1977) 'Cultural factors in spatial orientation,' in J. DOLGIN, D. KEMNITZER, & D. SCHNEIDER (Eds.) *Symbolic Anthropology: A Reader in the Study of Symbols and Meanings*, New York, Columbia University Press, 131–150.

HARKNESS, S. (1980) 'The cultural context of child development' in SUPER, C. and HARKNESS, S. (Eds.) *Anthropological Perspectives on Child Development*, Vol. 8, San Francisco, Jossey-Bass, pp. 7–14.

HARKNESS, S. and SUPER, C. (1980) 'Child development theory in anthropological perspective' in SUPER, C. and HARKNESS, S. (Eds.) *Anthropological Perspectives on Child Development*, Vol. 8, San Francisco, Jossey-Bass.

HASKINS, J. (1969) *Diary of a Harlem Schoolteacher*, New York, Grove Press.

HEATH, S. (1982) 'Questioning at home and at school: a comparative study' in SPINDLER, G. (Ed.) *Doing the Ethnography of Schooling: Educational*

Anthropology in Action, New York, Holt, Rinehart and Winston, pp. 102–31.

HEATH, S. (1983) *Ways with Words: Language, Life and Work in Communities and Classrooms* > Cambridge, Cambridge University Press.

HENRY, J. (1963) *Culture Against Man*, New York, Random House.

HERDON, J. (1968) *The Way It Spozed To Be*, New York, Simon and Schuster.

HESS, R. (1970) 'Social class and ethnic influences on socialization' in MUSSEN, P. (Ed.) *Carmichael's Manual of Child Psychology*, Vol. 2, 3rd edn, New York, John Wiley and Sons, pp. 457–557.

HESS, R. and SHIPMAN, V. (1965) 'Early experience and the socialization of cognitive modes in children', *Child Development*, 36, 4, pp. 869–86.

HILL, R. (1972) *The Strengths of Black Families*, New York, Emerson Hall.

HOWARD, A. and SCOTT, R. (1981) 'The study of minority groups in complex societies,' in R. MUNROE, R. MUNROE, & B. WHITING (Eds.) *Handbook of Cross-cultural Human Development*, New York, Garland STPM Press, 113–152.

HUNT, J. (1961) *Intelliguence and Experience*, New York, Ronald Press.

HUNT, J. (1964) 'The psychological basis for using preschool enrichment as an antidote for cultural deprivation', *Merrill-Palmer Quarterly of Behavior and Development*, 10, 3, July.

HUNT, J. (1969) *The Challenge of Incompetence and Poverty*, Urbana, University of Illinois Press.

HYMES, D. (1974) *Reinventing Anthropology*, New York, Vintage Books.

JENCKS, C. (1972) *Inequality: A Reassessment of the Effect of Family and Schooling in America*, New York, Basic Books.

JENSEN, A (1969) 'How much can we boost IQ and scholastic achievement?', *Harvard Educational Review*, 39, pp. 278–300.

JENSEN, A. (1972) *Genetics and Education*, New York, Harper and Row.

JOFFE, C. (1977) *Friendly Intruders: Child-care Professionals and Family Life*, Berkeley, Calif, University of California Press.

KAGAN, J. and MOSS, H. (1962) *Birth to Maturity, a Study of Psychological Development*, New York, Wiley.

KAGAN, J., MOSS, H. and SIGEL, I. (1963) 'Psychological significance of styles conceptualization', *Basic Cognitive Process in Children*, Society for Research in Child Development Monograph 86, Chicago, University of Chicago Press.

KARDINER, A. and LINTON, R. (1939) *The Individual and His Society*, New York, Columbia University Press.

KARNES, M., TESKA, J., HODGKINS, A. and BADGER, E. (1970) 'Educational intervention at home by mothers of disadvantaged infants', *Child Development*, 41, pp. 925–35.

KARWEIT, N. (1981) 'Time in school' in CORWIN, R. (Ed.) *Research in Sociology of Education and Socialization*, Greenwich, Conn, Jai Press.

KEDDIE, N. (1973) *Tinker, Tailor, The Myth of Cultural Deprivation*, Harmondsworth, Middx, Penguin Education.

KENISTON, K. and the CARNEGIE COUNCIL on CHILDREN (1977) *All Our Children: The American Family Under Pressure*, New York, Harcourt, Brace, Jovanovich.

KIRK, S. (1958) *Early Education for the Mentally Retarded*, Urbana, University of Illinois Press.

KOHL, H. (1967) *36 Children*, New York, The New American Library.

KOHLBERG, L. (1969) 'Stage and sequence: the cognitive developmental approach to socialization' in GOSLIN, D. (Ed.) *Handbook of Socialization Theory and Research*, Chicago, Rand McNally.

KOHN, M. (1959a) 'Social class and the exercise of parental authority', *American Sociological Review*, 24.

KOHN, M. (1959b) 'Social class and parental values', *American Journal of Sociology*, 24.

KOHN, M. (1963) 'Social class and parent-child relationships: an interpretation', *American Journal of Sociology*, 68, pp. 471–80.

KOZOL, J. (1967) *Death at an Early Age*, Boston, Houghton Mifflin.

KROEBER, A. and PARSONS, T. (1958) 'The concept of culture and of social system', *American Sociological Review*, 23, pp. 582–3.

LABOV, W. (1972) *Language in the Inner City: Studies in the Black English Vernacular*, Philadelphia.

LABOV, W. (1973) 'The logic of non-standard English' in KEDDIE, N. (Ed.) *Tinker, Tailor; The Myth of Cultural Deprivation*, Harmondsworth, Middx, Penguin Education.

LADNER, J. (1972) *Tomorrow's Tomorrow: the Black Woman*, New York, Anchor Books.

LADNER, J. (1973) 'The urban poor' in ROSE, P., ROTHMAN, S. and WILSON, W. (Eds.) *Through Different Eyes: Black and White Perspectives of American Race Relations*, New York, Oxford University Press, pp. 3–24.

LANGER, J. (1969) *Theories of Development*, New York, Holt, Rinehart and Winston.

LEACOCK, E. (1969) *Teaching and Learning in City Schools: A Comparative Study*, New York, Basic Books.

LEACOCK, E. (1971) *The Culture of Poverty: A Critique*, New York, Simon and Schuster.

LECOMPTE, M. and GOETZ, J. (1982) 'Problems of reliability and validity in ethnographic research', *Review of Educational Research*, 52, 1, spring, pp. 31–60.

LEE, D. (1980) 'Codifications of reality: lineal and non-lineal' in SPRADLEY, J. and McCURDY, D. (Eds.) *Conformity and Conflict: Readings in Cultural Anthropology*, Boston, Little, Brown, pp. 75–90.

LEIN, L. (1975) 'Black American migrant children: their speech at home and school. *Council on Anthropology and Education Quarterly*, 6, 1–11.

LESSER, G., FIFER, G. & CLARK, D. (1965) 'Mental abilities of children in different social class and cultural groups.' *Monographs of the Society for Research in Child Development*, 30, 647–.

LEVENSTEIN, P. (1979) 'Cognitive growth in preschoolers through verbal interaction with mothers.' *American Journal of Orthopsychiatry.*, 40, 3, 426–432.

LEVENSTEIN, P. (1972) 'But does it work in homes away from home?' *Theory into Practice*, 11, 3, 157–162.

LeVINE, R. (1970) 'Cross-cultural study in child psychology,' in P. MUSSEN (Ed.) *Carmichael's Manual of Child Psychology*, Vol. II, third edition, New York, John Wiley and Sons.

LEVI-STRAUSS, C. (1963) TOTEMISM (trans. by R. Needham). Boston, Beacon Press.

LEVI-STRAUSS, C. (1966) *The Savage Mind*. Chicago, University of Chicago Press.

LIEBOW, E. (1967) *Tally's Corner*. Boston, Little-Brown.

LINDBLOM, C. & COHEN, D. (1979) *Usable Knowledge: Social Science and Social Problem Solving*. New Haven, Yale University Press.

LUBECK, S. (1984) 'Kinship and classrooms: an ethnographic perspective on education as cultural transmission,' *Sociology of Education*, 57 (October), 219–232.

MACCOBY, E. and JACKLIN, C. (1974) *The Psychology of Sex Differences*, Stanford, Stanford University Press.

MADDEN, J., LEVENSTEIN, P. and LEVENSTEIN, S. (1976) 'Longitudinal IQ outcomes of the mother-child home program', *Child Development*, 47, pp. 1015–25.

MALINOWSKI, B. (1972a) *Argonauts of the Western Pacific*, London, George Routledge and Sons Ltd.

MALINOWSKI, B. (1972b) *The Father in Primitive Psychology*, New York, W. W. Norton.

McDAVID, J. *et al* (1965/67) *Project Head Start Evaluation and Research Summary*, Washington, DC, US Office of Economic Opportunity, Project Headstart, Division of Research and Evaluation.

MEAD, G. (1934) *Mind, Self and Society from the Standpoint of a Social Behaviorist*, Chicago, University of Chicago Press.

MEAD, M. (1930) *Growing Up in New Guinea*, New York, Morrow.

MEAD, M. (1931) 'The primitive child' in MURCHISON, C. (Ed.) *A Handbook of Child Psychology*, Worchester, Mass, Clark University Press.

MEAD, M. (1946) 'Research on primitive children' in CARMICHAEL, L. (Ed.) *Manual of Child Psychology*, New York, Wiley, pp. 735–80.

MEAD, M. (1971) 'Early childhood experience and later education in complex cultures' in WAX, M., DIAMOND, S. and GEARING, F. (Eds.) *Anthropological Perspectives on Education*, New York, Basic Books, pp. 67–90.

MEAD, M. (1976) 'Primitive education' in ROBERTS, J. and AKINSANYA, S. (Eds.) *Educational Patterns and Cultural Configurations*, New York, David McKay.

MEAD, M. and WOLFENSTEIN, M. (1955) *Childhood in Contemporary Cultures*, Chicago, University of Chicago Press.

MEHAN, H. (1978) 'Structuring school structure', *Harvard Educational Review*, 48, 1, February, pp. 32–64.

MINTURN, L. and LAMBERT, W. (1964) *Mothers of Six Cultures: Antecedents of Child Rearing*, New York, John Wiley and Sons.

MOORE, G., Jnr. (1976) 'Realities of the urban classroom' in ROBERTS, J. and AKINSANYA, S., (Eds.) *Schooling in the Cultural Context*, New York, David McKay, pp. 238–55.

MOYNIHAN, D. (1965) *The Negro Family: The Case for National Action*, prepared for the Office of Policy Planning and Research of the Department of Labor, Washington, DC.

NISBET, R. (1966) *The Sociological Tradition*, New York, Basic Books.

NISBET, R. (1974) *The Sociology of Emile Durkheim*, New York, Oxford University Press.

NOBLES, W. (1974) 'Africanity: its role in black families', *Black Scholar*, 5, 9, June, pp. 10–17.

OGBU, J. (1978) *Minority Education and Caste: The American System in Cross-cultural Perspective*, New York, Academic Press.

OGBU, J. (in press) 'Anthropology of education' in HUDSEN, T. and POSTLETH-WAITE, N. (Eds.) *International Encyclopedia of Education: Research and Studies*, Oxford, Pergamon Press Ltd.

OVERTON, W. and REESE, H. (1973) 'Models of development: methodological implications', in NESSELROD and REESE, H. (Eds.) *Life Span Developmental Psychology*, New York, Academic Press.

PALMER, F. and ANDERSON, L. (1979) 'Long-term gains from early intervention: findings from longitudinal studies' in ZIGLER, E. and VALENTINE, J. (Eds.) *Project Head Start: A Legacy of the War on Poverty*, New York, Free Press, pp. 433–66.

PARSONS, A. (1969) *Belief, Magic, and Anomie*, New York, Free Press.

PELTO, P. and PELTO, G. (1978) *Anthropological Research: The Structure of Inquiry*, New York, Cambridge University Press.

PESHKIN, A. (1978) *Growing Up American: Schooling and the Survival of Community*, Chicago, University of Chicago Press.

PETERS, M. (1981) 'Parenting in Black families with young children,' in H. McADOO (Ed.) *Black Families*, Beverly Hills, Sage Publications, 211–224.

PHILIPS, S. (1983) *The Invisible Culture: Communication in Classroom and Community on the Warm Springs Indian Reservation*, Research on Teaching Monograph Series, New York, Longman.

PHILLIPS, D. and KELLY, M. (1975) 'Hierarchical theories of development in education and psychology', *Harvard Educational Review*, 45, 3, August, pp. 351–75.

PIAGET, J. (1950) *The Psychology of Intelligence* (trans by M Piercy and D Berlyne), London, Routledge and Kegan Paul.

PIAGET, J. (1952) *The Origins of Intelligence in Children* (trans by M Cook), New York, International University Press.

PIAGET, J. (1970a) *Genetic Epistemology* (trans by E Duckworth), New York, W W Norton.

PIAGET, J. (1970b) 'Piaget's theory' in MUSSEN, P. (Ed.) *Carmichael's Manual of Child Psychology*, Vol. 1, New York, Wiley, pp. 703–32.

POWDERMAKER, H. (1966) *Stranger and Friend: The Way of an Anthropologist*, New York, W W Norton.

RAMIREZ, M. and PRICE-WILLIAMS, D. (1976) 'Achievement motivation in children of three ethnic groups in the United States', *Journal of Cross-cultural Psychology*, 7, pp. 47–60.

RICHMOND, J., STIPEK, D. and ZIGLER, E. (1979) 'A decade of Head Start' in ZIGLER, E. and VALENTINE, J. (Eds.) *Project Head Start: A Legacy of the War on Poverty*, New York, Free Press, pp. 135–54.

RIST, R. (1970) 'Student social class and teacher expectations: the self-fulfilling prophesy in ghetto education', *Harvard Educational Reivew*, 40, 3, August, pp. 411–51.

RIST, R. (1977) 'On the relations among educational research paradigms: from distain to detente', *Anthropology and Education Quarterly*, 8, 2, May, pp. 42–9.

RIST, R. (1978) *The Invisible Children: School Integration in American Society*, Cambridge, Mass, Harvard University Press.

ROBERTS, J. (1976) 'Introduction' in ROBERTS, J. and AKINSANYA, S. (Eds.) *Educational Patterns and Cultural Configurations*, New York, David McKay, pp. 1–20.

ROBERTS, J. and AKINSANYA, S. (Eds.) (1976a) *Educational Patterns and Cultural Configurations*, New York, David McKay.

ROBERTS, J. and AKINSANYA, S. (Eds) (1976b) *Schooling in the Cultural Context: Anthropological Studies of Education*, New York, David McKay.

RYAN, W. (1971) *Blaming the Victim*, New York, Pantheon Books.

SEARS, R. (1975) 'Your ancients revisited: a history of child development' in HETHERINGTON, E. (Ed.) *Review of Child Development Research*, Vol. 5, Chicago, University of Chicago Press, pp. 1–74.

SEARS, R., MACCOBY, E. and LEVIN, H. (1957) *Patterns of Child Rearing*, Evanston, Ill, Row, Peterson.

SELDEN, S. (1983) 'Biological determinism and the ideological roots of student classification', *Journal of Education*, 165, 2, spring, pp. 175–91.

SHADE, B. (1982) 'Afro-American cognitive style: a variable in school success', *Review of Educational Research*, 52, 2, summer, pp. 219–44.

SIGEL, I., ANDERSON, L. and SHAPIRO, H. (1966) 'Categorization behavior of lower and middle class pre-school children: differences in dealing with representation of familiar objects', *Journal of Negro Education*, 35, pp. 218–29.

SMITH, L. (1977) 'An evolving logic of participant observation, educational ethnography, and other case studies', *Review of Research in Education*, 6, pp. 316–77.

SMITH, L. (1978) 'Accident, anomalies, serendipity and making the commonplace problematic: the origins and evolution of the field study "problems"', paper presented at the Wingspread Conference on the Study of Schooling: Field Based Methodologies in Educational Research, Racine, Wisc, November (revised 1979).

SMITH, L. and GEOFFREY, G. (1968) *Complexities of an Urban Classroom*, New York, Holt, Rinehart and Winston.

SPIKER, C. (1970) 'The concept of development: relevant and irrelevant issues' in FITZGERALD, H. and McKINNEY, J. (Eds.) *Developmental Psychology: Studies in Human Development*, Homewood, Ill, Dorsey Press, pp. 4–18.

SPINDLER, G. (Ed.) (1955) *Anthropology and Education*, Stanford, Stanford University Press.

SPINDLER, G. (Ed.) (1963) *Education and Culture: Anthropological Approaches*, New York, Holt, Rinehart and Winston.

SPINDLER, G. (1974) 'Beth Ann: a case of culturally defined adjustment and teacher perception', in SPINDLER, G. (Ed.) *Education and Cultural Process: Toward an Anthropology of Education*, New York, Holt, Rinehart and Winston.

SPINDLER, G. (1982) (Ed.) *Doing the Ethnography of Schooling: Educational Anthropology in Action*, New York, Holt, Rinehart and Winston.

SPINDLER, G. (1982) 'Roger Harker and Schonhansen. 'From the familiar to the strange and back again' in SPINDLER, G. (Eds.) *Doing the Ethnography of Schooling: Educational Anthropology in Action*, New York, Holt, Rinehart and Winston, pp. 20–46.

SPIRO, M. (1982) *Oedipus in the Trobriands*, Chicago: University of Chicago Press.

STACK, C. (1974) 'Sex roles and survival strategies in an urban Black community' in ROSALDON, M. and LAMPHERE, L. (Eds.) *Women, Culture and Society*, Stanford, Stanford University Press, pp. 113–28.

STACK, C. (1975) *All our Kin: Strategies for Survival in a Black Community*, New York, Harper and Row.

STAPLES, R. (1974) 'The Black family revisited: A review and a preview', *Journal of Social and Behavioral Sciences*, 20, pp. 60–78.

STIPEK, D., VALENTINE, J. and ZIGLER, E. (1979) 'Project Head Start: a critique of theory and practice' in ZIGLER, E. and VALENTINE, J. (Eds.) *Project Head Start: A Legacy of the War on Poverty*, New York, Free Press, pp. 477–94.

SUDARKASA, N. (1981) 'Interpreting the African heritage in Afro-American family organization,' in H. McADOO (Ed.) *Black Families*. Beverly Hills, Sage Publications, 37–53.

SUPER, C. and HARKNESS, S. (Ed.) (1980) *Anthropological Perspectives on Child Development: New Directions for Child Development*, San Francisco, Jossey-Bass.

TALBERT, C. (1976) 'Interaction and adaptation in two Negro kindergartens' in ROBERTS, J. and AKINSANYA, S. (Eds.) *Educational Patterns and Cultural Configurations*, New York, David McKay, pp. 299–313.

TURNER, J. (1974) *The Structure of Sociological Theory*, Homewood, Ill, Dorsey Press.

VALENTINE, C. (1971) 'Deficit, difference, and bicultural models of Afro-American behavior', *Harvard Educational Review*, 41, 2, pp. 137–57.

WAX, M., DIAMOND, S. and GEARING, F. (Eds.) (1971) *Anthropological Perspectives on Education*, New York, Basic Books.

WAX, M. and WAX, R. (1963) 'Cultural deprivation as an educational ideology'. Paper presented at the 62nd Annual Meeting of the American Anthropological Association, November.

WAX, M. and WAX, R. (1971) 'Great tradition, little tradition and formal education' in WAX, M., DIAMOND, S. and GEARING, F. (Eds.) *Anthropological Perspectives on Education*, New York, Basic Books, pp. 3–18.

WAX, M. and WAX, R. (1980) 'Anthropological fieldwork: comments on its values and limitations', *Journal of Thought*, 15, 3, Fall, pp. 1–10.

WAX, M. WAX, R. and DUMONT, R. (1964) 'Formal education in an American Indian community', *Social Problems*, 11, 4.

WAX, R. (1971) *Doing Fieldwork: Warnings and Advice*, Chicago, University of Chicago Press.

WEIKART, D. and LAMBIE, D. (1967) 'Preschool intervention through a home teaching program' in HELLMUTH, J. (Ed.) *The Disadvantaged Child*, Vol. 2, Seattle, Special Child Publications.

WESTINGHOUSE LEARNING CORP (1969) *The Impact of Head Start: An Evaluation of the Effects of Head Start on Children's Cognitive and Affective Development*, Executive summary, Ohio University report to the Office of Economic Opportunity, Washington, DC, Clearinghouse for Federal Scientific and Technical Information, June.

WHITE, S. *et al* (1973) *Federal Programs for Young Children: Review and Recommendations*, Vol. 2, *Review of Evaluation Data for Federally Sponsored Projects for Children*, Cambridge, Mass, Huron Institute.

WHITING, B. (Ed.) (1963) *Six Cultures: Studies of Child Rearing*, New York, John Wiley and Sons.

WHITING, B. and WHITING, J. (1975) *Children of Six Cultures*, Cambridge, Harvard University Press.

WHITING, J. and CHILD, I. (1953) *Child Training and Personality: A Cross-cultural Study*, New Haven, Yale University Press.

WILCOX, K. (1982) 'Differential socializations in the classroom: implications for equal opportunity' and 'Ethnography as a methodology and its applications to the study of schooling: a review' in SPINDLER, G. (Eds.) *Doing the Ethnography of Schooling: Educational Anthropology in Action*, New York, Holt, Rinehart and Winston, pp. 268–309 and 456–88.

WILLIE, C. (1980) 'Family and kinship among black Americans' in SPRADLEY, J. and McCURDY, D. (Eds.) *Culture and Conformity: Readings in Cultural Anthropology*, Boston, Little, Brown, pp. 122–34.

WILLIE, C. (1981) *A New Look at Black Families*. Bayside, New York, General Hall, Inc.

WILLIS, P. (1981) *Learning to Labor*, New York, Columbia University Press.

WILSON, S. (1977) 'The use of ethnography techniques in educational research', *Review of Educational Research*, 47, 1, winter, pp. 245–65.

WOLCOTT, H. (1975) 'Criteria for an ethnographic approach to research in schools', *Human Organization*, 34, 2, pp. 111–27.

YOUNG, V. (1970) 'Family and childhood in a southern Georgia community', *American Anthropologist*, 72, pp. 269–88.

ZIGLER, E. and SEITZ, V. (1980) 'Early childhood intervention programs: a reanalysis', *Social Psychology*, 9, fall, pp. 354–68.

ZIGLER, E. and VALENTINE, J. (Eds.) (1979) *Project Head Start: A Legacy of the War on Poverty*, New York, Free Press.

ZIMMER, R. (1979) 'Necessary directions for anthropological research on child care in the United States', *Anthropology and Education Quarterly*, 10, 3, fall, pp. 139–65.

Author Index

Note: This index comprises names of authors cited in the text. In addition, users are referred to the comprehensive bibliography (pp. 147–58).

Abelson *et al.*, 11n9
Akinsanya, S.
  see Roberts and Akinsanya
Anderson, L.
  see Palmer and Anderson
Anyon, J., 5
Aron, R., 41n3

Baratz, S. and Baratz, J., 5, 7
Bauman, 47
Bear
  see Hess and Bear
Becker, H., 5, 81
Beller, 11n9
Benedict, R., 17, 18, 26, 38
Bernstein, B., 8, 10n5, 25, 139
Birdwhistell, R., 36, 44n17
Bloom, B., 4
Blumer, H., 17
Boas, 32
Bogdan, R. and Taylor, 48
Bowles, S. and Gintis, H., 5
Brainerd, C., 31
Bronfenbrenner, U., 24, 26, 51
Brophy, J., 4
Brown
  see Mercer and Brown
Bruner, J., 34, 80n3
  see also Greenfield and Bruner

Bruner, J. *et al.*, 28
Buck-Morss, S., 29, 44n16
Burnett, J., 35, 49, 50
Burt, C., 3
Burton, J. and Jones, L., 12n9
Byers, P. and Byers, H., 7, 36, 49

Caldwell, B., 10n5
Campbell, D.
  see Cook and Campbell
Campbell, D. and Stanley, J., 55
Carini, 52
Carnoy, M. and Levin, H., 9n4
Child, I.
  see Whiting and Child
Chomsky, N., 44n16
Cicierelli, V. *et al.*, 9n5
Cohen, D.
  see Lindblom and Cohen
Cohen, R., 7, 25, 34–5, 38–9, 45n21
Cohen, Y., 136
Cole, M.
  see Gay and Cole
Cole, M. and Gay, J., 32
Cole, M. *et al.*, 32–3
Condon, W. and Sander, L., 36
Cook, T. and Campbell, D., 55

Darwin, C., 9n1
Dasen, P., 28

Subject Index

ability
  and achievement, 3
abstract formalism, 44n16
  see also abstract thought;
    abstraction
abstract thought, 34–9, 40, 44n16,
  140
  see also abstract formalism;
    abstraction
abstraction, 29, 44n16, 106, 109, 136
  see also abstract formalism; abstract
    thought
achievement motivation, 28
activities
  in classrooms, 95–107, 134–6
adaptation
  to environment, 6, 13–40, 131,
    136–44 (and passim)
adult-collective model, 138, 141–3
adult-individualistic model, 136–40
Africa
  Kpelle in, 32–3
  Wolof in, 27, 34
Afro-Americans
  see also Black American children
  culture of, 39–40, 45n23
  family structure among, 5, see also
    kinship
Alaska, 45n20
Alor
  society in, 18–19
American Anthropological
  Association, 48
American Educational Research
  Association (AERA) Convention

(April 1983), 55
anthropological approach, passim
Anthropological Perspectives on
  Education, 48

Bali
  Mead's fieldwork in, 18
Bateson photographs, 18
behavior
  and child rearing practices, 14,
    28–31, 51ff
biological differences, 2–4
Black American children
  compared with White, passim
Black Americans
  in California, 80n7
  kinship among, see kinship
body movement, 36

California
  Black Americans in, 80n7
  studies of 'mental retardation' in,
    10n6
case study methodology, 47ff

CEMREL Inc., 58
charts
  of classroom activities, 52, 53, 55,
    57, 85, 88, 89, 91, 92

child-collective model, 142–3
child development
  see also Harmony preschool, child
    development at
  contexts of, 13–45

171